MAKING PALESTINE'S HISTORY
WOMEN'S TESTIMONIES

JEHAN HELOU

SPOKESMAN

*To a passionate advocate
and supporter of women's liberation
To my husband, Hanna Mikhail*

A larger edition was published in Arabic in 2009 by the
Palestinian Women's Research and Documentation Centre at UNESCO
This English translation of selections published in 2022 by
Spokesman
5 Churchill Park, Nottingham, NG4 2HF, England
spokesmanbooks.org
Spokesman is the publishing imprint of
The Bertrand Russell Peace Foundation Ltd.

A catalogue record is available from the British Library.

Printed and bound in Great Britain

ISBN 978 0 85124 905 6

CONTENTS

PREFACE

*Out of the Shadows: Palestinian women narrate their vital
role in making history*

*Personal testimonies of struggle and social transformation
1969-1984*

The history of the Palestinian Revolution is full of leaps and twists,
victories and defeats; it has many untold stories, rich and unique;
experiences not recorded, and not yet studied; experiences that will
disappear with those who lived them. What about the beginnings,
sacrifices, the initiatives, the ebb and flow? Much needs to be told,
much about the women revolutionaries, who, if they were
mentioned at all, it was only peripherally.

The Palestinian women's struggle in the National Liberation
Movement is intertwined with the struggle for women's liberation.
This book aims to give a voice to those women, the 'unknown
soldiers' of the Revolution, with their heroic struggle and bold
initiatives. These women were at times decision makers or
influenced the progress of the struggle despite the fact they were
denied leadership positions.

Few publications cover this subject – certainly not with the same
outlook, approach and with an active observer involved. These
testimonies are mainly the stories of the Nakba generation
spontaneously narrating their dispossession, suffering and heroic
struggle. These remarkable testimonies give them a voice not heard
before.

As I was part of the Palestinian National Liberation and women's

1

liberation struggle at the time, I believe it is our duty to document this rich experience. The main documents of the General Union of Palestinian Women (GUPW) were lost during the Israeli aggression in 1982. I tried to meet this challenge through higher studies at Birkbeck College, London University; unfortunately, financial and personal reasons halted that. This is how I started to search for other means to accomplish what has become a national duty.

The idea started to grow with me of the importance of recording – before memory is lost and the body gone – the rich and distinguished experiences of Palestinian women in Lebanon, women who contributed to their people's honourable history. The project started in 1993-1994 but was interrupted for personal and objective reasons, and resumed in 2007. I conducted and recorded 53 interviews and had them transcribed. The resulting testimonies were based on personal live interviews, inspired by oral history technique as the best method of documenting the untold part of people's history.

The narrators were mostly women leaders and cadres of the General Union of Palestinian Women – General Secretariat and of the Lebanese Branch – drawn from the different political factions. They were mainly women who struggled at grassroots level and played an important role in defending the Revolution and empowering and mobilizing thousands of women. Moreover there was a very interesting roundtable discussion with women cadres based in South Lebanon about their experience after the Israeli invasion and occupation in 1982. Each interviewee had the full space to tell her story: the process of transformation, personal difficulties and achievements, and her position on related issues of social change. Different angles of broad questions were covered according to the individual's experience. Each testimony is published as told with minor editing to avoid repetition and retain accuracy.

I opted to interview cadres and leaders of GUPW because it

covers their grassroots struggle mostly in crisis situations as well as their projects and work among women. Organizational work and political issues inside different Palestinian factions were rarely addressed, though most interviewees belonged to the different groups.

These testimonies formed the book published in Arabic in 2009 by UNESCO through the Palestinian Women's Research and Documentation Center in the Occupied Palestinian Territory. The book was launched in Palestine, Lebanon and Jordan and was well reviewed in Arabic newspapers. Extracts were translated and published in English

I personally conducted all interviews. I was part of the struggle on both grassroots and leadership levels and I knew most of the interviewees and could check the accuracy of the information. This facilitated the interviewees' quick response and cooperation. I thank them wholeheartedly for their willing cooperation and warm encouragement that provided me with the incentive to complete the work despite tremendous difficulties.

Publishing this English edition has been a long and thorny task. Translating from colloquial Arabic was demanding and needed to be checked thoroughly before the draft was sent to a patient and professional editor. The translation took two years to prepare. This English edition is based on the Arabic one and includes 17 of the most important testimonies. It is edited to keep answers as narrated (my questions and unnecessary details omitted) with further work by a professional editor. A short profile introducing each interviewee is included. There are excerpts from three important testimonies by leading women whose experiences in the struggle have been published by others. It was vital to include the testimony of the Director of the GUPW Institute for the Children of Martyrs (BAS) for its richness.

We hope this book will become part of the literature recording the international heritage of national liberation movements and women's liberation struggles. It is a rich resource for research and analysis. I genuinely hope this book will motivate research centres to support further studies of the various aspects of this rich experience of Palestinian women.

Jehan Helou
February 2022

INTRODUCTION
Jehan Helou

The oral testimonies of Palestinian women presented here shed light on a vital part of history until now ignored. Palestinian women played a prominent role in the Palestinian Revolution in Lebanon (1969-1982). They had to contend on several fronts during the long struggle for Palestinian national liberation: against Zionism, colonialism, imperialism, and reactionary Arab regimes and forces, as well as against social injustice and a patriarchal system that enslaved them and degraded their humanity.

Documentation about this important role fades with the passage of time and the accumulation of tremendous political change and crises. However, the question arises as to why this honourable role in making history has remained in the shadows. Is it not a crucial part of Palestinian history and of women's liberation struggle around the world? Surely knowledge of this history helps an understanding of the current situation of the Palestinian people in general, and of their struggle in Occupied Palestine and Lebanon.

This forgotten story is told by the interviewees recorded in this book, each one narrating her complex struggle and the importance of social transformation. Here are the voices of revolutionary women, narrating their outstanding experiences at different stages in their lives; their struggle with their parents and society and their joining the revolution. In this important oral history, we read of rich experiences never recounted before. These courageous voices tell how women seized their role in the revolution and began their liberation process, not depending on the impetus of the

5

revolutionary situation alone, or on the encouragement of their male compatriots, but as pioneers grabbing every opportunity to be in the forefront of the national struggle, boldly breaking the chains that enslaved them. They had a remarkable role in the progress of the revolution, and in defending it.

Great sacrifices were made, initiatives courageously taken, and landmarks accomplished. It is striking and heart-warming to read women's narratives delivered spontaneously with all humility, reflecting that their sacrifices for their homeland were natural. They never expected recognition but were glad to tell their story to the world; that of breaking their chains and their struggle for their liberation and their right to be part of the decision-making echelons.

The revolutionary atmosphere was the catalyst. Though the PLO had no central vision or programme addressing women's issues, women persisted and escalated their struggle and sacrifices. Vanguard women tore up the oppressive traditions, broke out of their cage and introduced their own conventions and norms, thus taking control of their lives. The direct connection between women's liberation and national liberation is obvious in women's experiences in Jordan, Lebanon, and the Occupied Territory. These leaps forward and social transformations were the beginning of Palestinian women's liberation, though, for both objective and subjective reasons, no change took place in family status law. Moreover, there was a shameful absence of women in the leadership positions, despite women's vital role and sacrifices.

Unfortunately, the Palestinian Revolution was aborted by its permanent trio of enemies: Israel, imperialism, and Arab reactionary forces – mainly through the Israeli aggression on Lebanon in 1982. The military and political leadership and members had to leave Lebanon. The PLO had also lost its socio-economic existence. However, the national struggle did not end; as long as colonialism and injustice are present, the spirit of the

Introduction

Revolution inhabits the Palestinian people.

Women's struggle for their liberation goes on. In their testimonies some women call this period the 'Golden Age', and they all describe it as the best time of their lives – lives that were transformed by the Revolution. Though the process of women's liberation at the grassroots level and the formalizing of the laws guaranteeing gender equality were halted, women's rich experience, empowerment and social consciousness cannot be reversed. Palestinian women generally were empowered and, as we read in the profiles and testimonies, hundreds of them have become 'new women'. Despite the fact that women in the oppressed Palestinian camps lost many of their socio-economic benefits, the majority were empowered; they join in the defence of their camps against all attacks and play an important role in protest at the racist policies imposed on the Palestinian refugees.

EPISODES

History is full of episodes of human suffering inflicted by systems of oppression and subjugation, whether it is slavery, colonialism, racism, or any other form of oppression, with women enduring these doubly. All these systems were patriarchal and enforced the marginalization of women and the supremacy of men. The struggle of men and women around the world against oppression and domination has never stopped. The national and women's liberation struggles have always been correlated and have inspired women's movements around the world. Each struggle, as well as the post-independence situation, was unique. Most of these stories have been narrated and retold, aiming to enrich women's struggle and ignite the candle of hope.

Women's issues and their fight for emancipation and justice have had different names at different times*. In this book I chose the term in use in the period under review, that of women's

7

liberation. Maybe the word 'liberation' resonated in our ears, and indeed this is how we understood feminism: women breaking the chains of subjugation, and the centuries-old taboos and traditions.

The Palestinian feminist movement was born in the early 1920s out of the womb of national liberation struggle against British colonialism and Zionist settlement. However, the important social changes came only with the Palestinian Revolution. Understanding the socio-political aspects of Palestinian history is essential to grasping the current complicated situation of Palestinians inside occupied Palestine and in exile. Women had a major role in the growth of the Revolution, in securing its steadfastness and in facing attempts to liquidate it. After the Israeli invasion of Lebanon and the withdrawal of fighters and cadres from the country in 1982, women assumed practical leadership.

These testimonies reveal some important issues, such as how Palestinian women were a vital part of the Palestinian Revolution despite being excluded from the echelons of leadership; the democratic process in the Revolution; reflections on the great social transformation in their lives and in women's situation in general, despite there were no changes to family law and the legal system. The testimonies reveal how new, unwritten revolutionary social norms, values and practices started to emerge, affecting the lives of thousands of women; but, most importantly, why the process of women's liberation was aborted.

These testimonies challenge the classical measure of women's percentage in leadership roles as the main criterion for judging their influence and role in affecting decision making, demonstrating that in a revolution and in people's struggle and steadfastness reality can be different.

*The term 'gender' is more accurate since it affirms the social and cultural differences between the two sexes, and not the biological ones.

A Glimpse at the Roots of the Palestinian People's Dispossession

The Palestinian people have been waging their national struggle against British colonialism and Zionist settler colonialism since the Balfour Declaration (1917). This was a British colonialist declaration stating that the British government viewed with favour *'the establishment in Palestine of a national home for the Jewish people'* and would *'use their best endeavours to facilitate the achievement of this object'*. The British did not honour the second part of the declaration which stated: *'it being clearly understood that nothing shall be done which may prejudice the civil and religious rights of existing non-Jewish communities in Palestine'*.

Uprooting of Palestinians from their homeland by coercion and massacres in 1948 has become a saga. The tragedy of their dispossession could not have taken place without the full support and collaboration of Britain and the United States with the Zionist movement and state. In 1914-1915 Jews constituted some 5.37% of the population (McCarthy); in 1947, following all the waves of Jewish immigration since the Balfour Declaration, Jews constituted one-third of the population (Pappe) and owned less than 6% of the land (McDowall). The ideal solution at that time was for Jews and Arabs to live on an equal basis in a democratic state. But this was not the policy of the Zionist organization, which wanted a pure Jewish state, a colonial base for the imperialist powers.

The struggle and steadfastness of the Palestinian people were outstanding, but they had limited means to face the superior power of the colonialists and invaders. Many massacres and civilian killings were committed with the aim of uprooting Palestinians and ethnically cleansing in order to leave the land for the Zionists. Israel completely demolished and depopulated around 400 villages in 1948 and many more since. Some 800,000 Palestinians became refugees and remained so, with Israel's rejection of UN resolution

194, repeated at every UN session, calling for their return. Only 120,000 Palestinians were allowed to remain in Palestine, where they became second class citizens in a state proclaimed 'the state of the Jewish people'. Any Jew has the right of return no matter where s/he is, while Palestinian refugees cannot return to their homeland. The Israeli Palestinians have 'been subject to systematic and widespread discrimination — socio-economic and "fundamentally political" discrimination' (McDowall 1989).

PALESTINIANS IN LEBANON

As a result of the disaster – the 'Nakba' of 1948 — and uprooting of most of the Palestinian people (800,000) from their land, around 100,000 Palestinian refugees came to Lebanon, mostly from the villages of Northern Palestine. Leaving behind their homes, their belongings and all they possessed and loved, they ended up in camps with atrocious conditions where they had to endure deprivation and oppression. Most Palestinian refugees (hundreds of thousands) outside the Occupied Palestinian Territory (OPT) are in Jordan, Syria, Lebanon and, until 1991, Kuwait. The most deprived and exposed to violations of human rights are the Palestinians in Lebanon.

Historically, the Lebanese state kept an iron grip on the Palestinian refugee camps, which were like ghettoes, denied any civil or human rights. This was mainly because the Lebanese political system is based on religious factionalism and controversy regarding the population's national identity. This lay behind the outbreak of the Lebanese civil war in 1975 when the right wing forces were alarmed at the change in the balance of power to the advantage of the Lebanese progressive forces that also supported the Palestinian Revolution.

The Palestinian refugees were distributed over 17 camps in Lebanon (Sayigh); refugees coming from the same village opted to be together. They lived in tents in horrendous conditions before moving to what resembled houses, some of which were incomplete with just a ceiling of tin or zinc. The camps had no infrastructure or major services, the inhabitants deprived of the basic needs for a dignified life. A machine of oppression was controlling their lives, limiting their movement and depriving them of any career or work, in addition to forbidding them any political activity.

There were also Palestinian refugees living in poverty outside the camps. Some of the Palestinian middle and professional classes were able to transmit their expertise to Lebanon, thus contributing effectively to the building of the Lebanese economy in the 1950s and '60s. However, all Palestinians were united through the secret political activities in the pan-Arab parties they joined, hoping to realize their dreams of liberating and returning to Palestine, as well as to bring closer the dream of Arab unity as a means to that end.

The 'Deuxieme Bureau', the Lebanese Intelligence Service, was very repressive. It monitored the smallest details of refugee lives. Even when people stayed up late at night they would hear a knock at the door from the Deuxieme Bureau: 'what radio station are you listening to, what are you talking about?'

If we wanted to hammer in a nail or build something we had to get the agreement of the 'Deuxieme Bureau'
Hamda Iraqi

THE EMERGENCE OF THE PALESTINIAN REVOLUTION

With the occupation of the rest of Palestine and part of the Egyptian and Syrian lands in 1967, the Contemporary Palestinian National Movement (CPNM) or Palestinian Revolution (as it was termed at the time) grew into a popular movement, gaining the support of the Palestinian and Arab peoples. The Palestinians were convinced that popular armed struggle was the most effective means to face

11

the powerful Israeli occupation army with its advanced and destructive weapons.

Thousands of young Palestinians and hundreds of Arabs quickly joined the Palestinian resistance, which started to build its main base in Jordan in 1968, and to a smaller degree in Lebanon. The Palestine Liberation Organization (PLO) was transformed into a national front representing the minimum national consensus and gaining worldwide support and recognition. In 1970-71, following the Jordanian regime's attack on and, later, liquidation of the Palestinian Resistance (PR), an attack known as Black September, the Revolution lost its main base in Jordan and moved to Lebanon.

The majority of Lebanese people supported the Palestinian cause and revolution. A joint leadership committee was established to confront Israeli aggression on Lebanese villages and the Palestinian camps and to face the Lebanese fascists who instigated the civil war and were represented by the Phalangists who later led the Lebanese Front.

In 1969 all the Palestinian refugee camps rose up to expel the hated Deuxieme Bureau, and women barricaded with their bodies the entrances to the camps to prevent the entry of Lebanese tanks. (I was an eyewitness.) Subsequently, the Cairo Agreement was signed between the PLO and the army and this regulated the presence and activities of guerrillas in South Lebanon. The refugee camps were placed under the authority of the Palestinians.

This in itself was a revolution. The Palestinian Revolution had great authority in the camps and it became a quasi state, building its institutions and offering many services to its people. Yet, it never developed into a comprehensive revolution as it had a weak social context. Unfortunately, the revolution faced brutal attempts to liquidate it, beginning with the outbreak of Lebanese civil war in which the Palestinian resistance and the Lebanese national and progressive forces jointly defeated the fascists and protected the independence of Lebanon and the Palestinian Revolution.

At this point the Israelis, with the support of the imperialists and the reactionary Arab forces, began their bloody and destructive attacks on Lebanon and the Palestinians and, in 1982, Israel invaded Lebanon. Thousands were killed and wounded; cities, villages and Palestinian camps were completely or extensively destroyed. The steadfastness of the Lebanese and Palestinian people in the face of the ruthless Israeli-American weapons, banned under Geneva Conventions, gained the admiration and solidarity of the world. However, they faced huge military superiority and a ruthlessness that violated human rights and international law. Eventually, the revolution was defeated, though the struggle did not end; the military and political leadership and members had to withdraw from Lebanon, and the fascists gained control for a short time.

PALESTINIAN WOMEN'S STRUGGLE IN THE REVOLUTION

Palestinian women joined their people's national struggle in the face of the dangers that had encircled their homeland since the early 1920s. Women supported the movement to stop land grabbing by Zionists, they supported the families of martyrs and detainees, and they supported the freedom fighters, smuggling arms and ammunition to their bases in villages and the mountains.

In 1921, in order to organize and make their voices heard, Palestinian women founded the Women's Union. Its first conference took place in 1929. Women also participated in the Palestinian revolution of 1936-1939 in the mass resistance against the British Mandate and Zionist settlements. They were pioneers who challenged norms and traditions.

During the bitter years of the Nakba (1948-67) (literally 'catastrophe' referring to the Palestinians' uprooting from their homeland), Palestinian refugees faced tremendous suffering, but additional oppression was imposed on women. Palestinians held strongly to the old traditions, the positive as well as the reactionary, only accepting social change very slowly, and this impacted badly on women, prolonging their subordination. Palestinians' main concern was to fight all attempts to liquidate them as a people and to defend their national identity at a time when there was no resistance movement as such. Women in general were the main victims of this tendency, since laws and traditions, which derived some legitimacy from religion and the patriarchal system, subordinated them. The issue of gender equality was not a public issue at all.

However, Palestinian mothers were instrumental in holding out against all odds and in facing the horrors of the Nakba, keeping the social fabric together, and cherishing national identity and the right of return. The mother retained her power within the family, but as usual in such societies, because of external challenges and powerlessness, she upheld and defended the conservative traditions and, moreover, required the acquiescence of the younger generation, especially her daughters.

Palestinians in the camps held on to their identity. We must not forget that there is a distinguished role of women ...

Bayan Nuwayhed al-Hout

Before the Revolution, the age for marriage ranged between 13 and 15 years ... the marriage would be arranged by the parents, inflicting injustice on both sides ...

Muyassar Ismail

WOMEN'S ROLE IN THE PALESTINIAN REVOLUTION

For Palestinians in Lebanon, the Revolution embodied more than a dream: to liberate Palestine and free the refugees from repressive Lebanese security and miserable living conditions in the camps. The camps became the main reservoir of the Revolution. For women this provided a third dimension to their liberation process: it was the magic that ejected the genie from its bottle and brought the dream of liberation to reality. The liberation of the camps was a leap forward in women's situation and their participation in the struggle and defence of the camps. A few days after the camp uprising, women started to receive military training and joined in guarding their camp to make sure the army did not return. But soon after, the process took a slower turn. Women began to join the ranks, but initially only a few of them. The tight social norms made it difficult for a woman to become active: politics and a public presence were only for men, she could only be supportive. The struggle of vanguard women was on two levels: the national struggle and the struggle with their families and society. Girls capitalised on their parents' national sentiment and their belief in the resistance.

We would not go out except with our parents ... at the beginning people and society did not view the girls who participated very positively.

Amneh Suleiman

Intissar al-Wazir affirms that Fatah, initially, did not have a unified vision on the role of women. *There were two currents inside the Fatah movement. One believed in the role of women within the movement and the other that she should work only at home.* (The latter was weaker.)

Vanguard women defied norms, broke their chains, and started

15

to dig their way out, participating in all aspects of the struggle, including some military activities. Many women became role models for both women and men. The rapid transformation of the Revolution into a broad popular movement made the pace of change tremendous. People were no longer afraid of getting rid of reactionary traditions and replacing them with revolutionary and progressive values, since these seemed to enhance their national identity and the Revolution, as well as their vital interests. This had been manifested also in Jordan in 1968-70. In the Occupied Palestinian Territory it began with the early stages of the struggle against the Israeli occupation and gained momentum during mass protests and demonstrations and, of course, during the popular Intifada in 1987.

From the beginning of 1968, many women pressed for military training to join the Fedayeen, seeing this as the best response to the bitter defeat. Women left home to go to Amman or Kayfoon or Mukhtara in Lebanon to join the training camps; in the same way as Palestinian women in the occupied territory were involved in armed activities against the Israeli occupation. Women started to become a separate entity, moving from being mothers, wives, sisters and daughters to being activists on the same terrain as men. They joined the different political factions and participated in organization and mobilization. At the beginning this was spontaneous and limited mainly to middle-class women living outside the camps. Later it started to develop into a grassroots movement more radicalized and aggressive. Like all liberation movements, the Revolution in general was supportive of the women's struggle, since it helped in promoting its own goals; initiatives were encouraged by the slogan 'Let a hundred flowers bloom!' Still, many of the leaders perceived women's role as supportive and supplementary rather than as one of equality. Such changes needed time but the women pioneers were not about to wait.

Introduction

Hundreds of women joined the different political factions, which concentrated on raising political and social awareness, organizing other women, and promoting their participation in the national struggle. However, most of the grassroots mobilization and organization was through the General Union of Palestinian Women (GUPW). The GUPW was the main women's organization that included all political factions and was affiliated to the PLO; it was established in Jerusalem a year after the PLO was founded. It was the umbrella organization for the women's movement, with its temporary headquarters in Beirut. It was underground in the Occupied Palestinian Territory and had branches in most Arab countries. Regular GUPW activities responded directly to the needs of women and children and defending the Revolution. In 1976 GUPW established 'Home' project for children of the martyrs of Tal al-Za'atar: BAS — Home of Steadfastness for the Children of Martyrs. The Lebanese branch founded kindergartens in almost every camp and started initiatives to help working women by establishing nurseries and subsidized restaurants. Moreover, it had a very successful literacy campaign. GUPW assumed the main role in providing the means for steadfastness during emergencies by preparing shelters and first aid centres, distributing food and supplies, and caring for the wounded and families of martyrs.

The participation of women was spontaneous and massive when there was any threat, aggression, or siege of the Palestinian camps. They organized daily emergency plans to help in defending and guarding the camp.

Hundreds of Lebanese women joined the Revolution, either with the Palestinian factions or through their own Lebanese political parties and women's organizations, and many Lebanese women participated in the GUPW. The participation grew during emergencies. A Lebanese/Palestinian Women's Preparatory

17

Committee was formed to work at the political and popular levels, reflecting the solidarity of the two peoples.

The GUPW called a meeting to confront the attack on the bus... This meeting was a turning point. More than three hundred Palestinian and Lebanese sisters came to the Union's headquarters

Rima Bordcosh

HIGHLIGHTS OF WOMEN'S STRUGGLE

Women's national and gender struggles are manifest in their oral testimonies. Their participation transformed their social situation, empowering them and enabling their liberation. Here we address popular struggle, we do not address the political and organizational role of women in the different Palestinian factions.

LANDMARKS AND INITIATIVES

The landmarks and initiatives cited briefly below show how women made heroic choices that promoted their struggle in response to the needs and priorities of the period. Women chose to work in unity, standing up to the leadership when necessary. They traversed dangerous roads to reach the besieged Tal al Za'atar camp, participated in the fighting in the 'hot' areas, and faced Israeli invasion and siege. Their initiatives helped heal the wounds after the siege of Tal al Za'atar, the Sabra and Shatila massacres, and the destruction of Ein al-Hilweh camp.

IMPORTANCE OF NATIONAL UNITY

The organizational structure of both the GUPW General Secretariat and the Lebanese branch, in advance of other unions and syndicates, was based on a coalition of all the Palestinian factions (similar to PLO representation), reflecting faith in the importance of national unity in the national struggle. The PLO was a coalition of different factions that had its shortcomings but served well during political consensus. This national cooperation was instrumental in elevating the Revolution and promoting the role of women within it.

From 1973 to 1982 women's work advanced, the main reason being the national unity evident at the time.

Samira Salah

I prefer group and women's union work to organizational work — when you are dealing with people who think differently from you, you benefit more.

Hamda Iraqi

My convictions were strengthened through our experience in the Lebanon branch: that common daily work shortens the distance between women of the factions, and contributes to building healthy national relations based on respect, creating space for dialogue…

Majida Masri

We were facing a social catastrophe which required unified efforts … I consider that the women in the camp were a guarantee against many collisions among the factions…

Amneh Suleiman

POLITICAL INDEPENDENCE AND CONTENTION

The General Union of Palestinian Women tried to preserve its political independence on major issues despite being one of the bases of the PLO. This was not easy as the GUPW depended financially on the PLO, but it managed to stand firm at points of important political contention. One important stand against a PLO political decision required a day-and-a-half extension of the Second Congress of the Women's Union in 1974. The majority of the Congress would not comply with the leadership's wishes to guarantee full support for the National Council decision (it was not unanimous) agreeing to the provisional programme known then as the 'Ten Points', which called for establishing an authority/state on any liberated land of Palestine. Despite many meetings the leadership held, especially with the Congress's Fatah members, the majority insisted on restrictions to this provisional programme before accepting it, in order to ensure that Palestinian national rights were not compromised, and that it would not constitute a step towards an unfair settlement or even surrender. In the end the Women's Congress agreed to the addition of the establishment of a national authority on any liberated land, provided that it did not contradict the PLO's National Pact, which called for the liberation of the whole of the land of Palestine. In response to this action of the women's union, the late leader Abu Ammar froze the activities of the GUPW General Secretariat for six months!

The Congress considered this an acceptance of the political compromise and an abandonment of the programme of total liberation.

Mai Sayegh

Introduction

The GUPW played an important role internationally, forging relations with women in liberation movements, progressive forces, socialist countries and UN agencies. The Soviet Women's Committee offered the GUPW 30 university scholarships for Palestinian girls in exile and from the Occupied Territory. It also attained high positions in the Women's International Democratic Federation and the Pan-Arab Women's Federation.

One of the main achievements of the GUPW was its important role in initiating and passing the first UN resolution condemning Zionism as a racist movement. This took place during the meeting held in Mexico in 1975. It was later approved by the UN General Assembly that same year.

... It saw the first established Palestinian victory. We cannot forget the withdrawal of the Arab, Muslim, African, non-aligned and socialist states from the auditorium at the beginning of the Israeli delegation's speech.

Issam Abdel Hadi

The UN Women's Conference ... unfortunately, this was later rescinded because our leadership policies did not keep up these achievements.

Amal Masri

INITIATIVES AND HEROISM

Most initiatives were not part of a larger plan or organizational order. Women cadres played an important role in the steadfastness and resistance of Tal al-Za'atar camp, which was besieged by Lebanese fascist forces for 76 days. Masses of ordinary women struggled heroically and sacrificed in defence of their camp and its

21

steadfastness. The outstanding testimonies reveal the courage of those women who, on their own initiative, chose to enter the camp at the height of the siege.

When I used to cross from West Beirut to Tal al-Za'atar I was risking my life because of kidnappers, snipers.

Shadia Helou

I asked permission of the director of Central Operations, Abu al-Walid. He refused, but I insisted. It was a harsh journey up the mountain roads.

Hamda Iraqi

The experience in 1982 in the southern area of Beirut, which was heavily targeted by the Israeli army from land, sea and air, is remarkable. Representatives of the international organizations providing supplies said, *'where do you get the nerves to endure work under such circumstances?'* (Fadia and Amal)

After 1982, almost all the male cadres had withdrawn from Lebanon with the PLO or were imprisoned by Israel or the pro-fascist Lebanese forces and army. There were further huge problems for the Palestinians in Lebanon as the PLO stopped sending money for their subsistence. The local leadership of the GUPW in each camp and quarter did a remarkable job, despite the fact that they were completely isolated from headquarters. Women cadres had to take over and follow up the overwhelming social problems, comfort those who had lost loved ones, and take care of the wounded, the detainees, and those who had lost their homes or incomes. They put themselves in danger when obtaining salaries for the families of the martyrs and prisoners. The Sabra and Shatila massacres were a traumatic and shocking event, and the women had to deal with the ensuing tremendous loss and suffering. Bayan saw the need to document these dreadful events.

I felt that the tragedy was far greater than reported. So after a few meetings I started recording the testimonies.
Bayan Nuwayhed al-Hout

The testimonies of women from South Lebanon in the 'Round Table' and of Muyassar Ismail narrate remarkable initiatives and heroism in facing the Israeli onslaught and occupation. We read how Palestinian women alone rebuilt Ain al-Hilweh camp, which had been flattened (all the houses destroyed) like a playground by the Israelis.

This is a big change for woman: she became both man and woman, responsible for the house, building it, and providing for its needs. The resistance came, but there were no plans for how people would persevere.
Round table - Kananah Rahmeh

After the invasion, the UNRWA brought tents to Ain al-Hilweh. The uprising was from us women. We refused. A group of us was formed and each brought a bottle of gasoline and burned all the tents. We did not have any men at all ... we built with our hands. This was the first uprising of women.
Round table - Umm Amer

It is remarkable how women saved the camp of Miyye wa Miyye with their initiatives and persistence:

We were stubborn and refused to go ... There was no food, we would go back to the fridges and bring food; there were no sandbags, we would make sacks and fill them with sand; the weapons needed cleaning ...
Round table - Basma Antar

I always say that these women, who are the mothers of the martyrs, are the unknown soldiers. These women provided food for the camp, gasoline for the hospital, medicines, clothes, and sometimes money, as it was forbidden for anyone to leave the camp.

Amneh Suleiman

During the war on the camps, the Lebanese Amal movement, supported by the Syrian regime, wanted to control the Palestinians in the camps and their political decision-making.

CONSCIOUSNESS RAISING AND LITERACY CAMPAIGNS

The different factions gave importance to political education. The General Secretariat and its Lebanese branch had a good consciousness-raising programme, educating its cadres on women's issues and the political situation. The GUPW had a prominent role in establishing libraries and promoting reading; lectures played an important role in consciousness-raising.

If the woman was working, we would go to the house and help her with her work so that she could come to the literacy class… It was one hundred per cent successful.

Kananah Rahmeh

What a delight to see women writing letters to their sons at the Fedayeen base!

Rima Bordcosh

The GUPW General Secretariat published the occasional newsletter and political communiqué responding to political junctures. However, it failed to have a Union magazine which would have contributed to elevating the political, social and educational awareness of women. The Union's leadership was not determined enough to find a way to overcome the obstructions of the PLO leadership, which was not in favour of allowing the Women's Union an independent platform.

ROLE IN THE MILITARY STRUGGLE

When women joined the resistance movement their main aim was to become freedom fighters. The slogan of the Revolution at the time was 'Armed struggle is the road to liberate Palestine' — inspired by Algeria and Vietnam as the best response to Zionist colonization and aggression.

From the outset, some vanguard women campaigned for military training to join the Fedayeen. Women left home for Amman, Kayfoon, or Mukhtara in Lebanon to join training camps, with the aim of crossing to the Occupied Territory. In addition, Palestinian women in the Occupied Territory started to be involved in underground armed activities against the Israeli occupation. Some of them became martyrs and others were imprisoned for many years.

It attracted 400 students from all universities not just one, and there were Lebanese and Arabs. The war broke out in June (1967) and we joined in July.

Hasna Rida

The participation of women in the struggle [in Jordan] at higher levels became more acceptable socially and so they began arms training, going to military camps and sleeping outside the home.

Wadad Qomri

Women in the different factions were required to have military training. There was training in each locality, or centrally, with special camps for women. Many were trained in Syria before the start of the Lebanese civil war. They pioneered an effective role in this field where their experiences in military training camps exposed them to bombs and rockets, and they persisted.

Few women joined the Fedayeen bases in South Lebanon; the social situation there did not allow for wide participation. However, reality imposed itself. With the outbreak of the Lebanese civil war, the need grew for locally based military units (known as militia) to defend the Revolution by protecting the camp and its neighbourhood, at the expense of military operations inside the Occupied Territory. Some women went to fight outside their locality, mostly in strategic areas such as the hotels district in Beirut, where there was heavy fighting, or on the front lines in Shiyah.

I had had some training on anti-aircraft guns ... But I did not think women should join the military bases in South Lebanon ... we had military patrols ... the minimum was about seventy-five women

Amal Masri

The military training of women developed and women began to participate militarily — especially after the Tal al-Zaatar massacre.

Samira Salah

Some women worked in the wireless section of military operations.

Nadia was killed while working in the wireless section in the Sanaya building in 1982.

Hamda Iraqi

Though many bombs fell around Bir Hassan camp, the girls were

able to complete the training ... Abu Ammar suggested establishing a women's military division and having women guards. We did not agree to this, as we felt that it wasn't a serious suggestion — women should not just be for decoration.
Shadia Helou

Women did not ask for recognition but wanted to be a vital part of the Revolution. During the Israeli invasion of Lebanon and the siege of Beirut in 1982, women played an important military role. Civilians from Burj al-Shimali, men, women and children, old and young, joined with the military to defend their camp.

More than 30 military vehicles were destroyed at the entrances to the camp and the Israeli commander of the operation was killed.
Muyassar Ismail

We trained on mortars and the quadruple [machine gun] ... two days after the invasion they (Israelis) had reached Sidon and we saw the tanks. It took a month for Ain al-Hilweh camp to fall.
Round Table - Amal Shihabi

It is remarkable how women's military role challenged the stereotypical image men had of women. It shook up many of the traditional values and men realized that women could be their equals in all fields. This perception was strengthened by women activists inside the Occupied Territory such as Shadia Abu Ghazaleh, Fatima Bernawi, Aisha and Rasmieh Oudeh. The operation led by the young Martyr Dalal Moughrabi broke the taboos.

ROLE IN NATIONAL COUNCIL AND LEADERSHIP

Although some women reached leadership positions in later years in some leftist organizations and in Fatah, and also in some PLO departments and institutions, the ratio to that of men was dismal. The PLO did open the way for women's involvement in response to their participation in the national struggle, but the proportion of women on the National Council (NC) reached only 7.5% (it was 3% when the PLO was founded). There was no woman on the PLO Executive Committee till 2009. Even in the wider circles of the PLO the participation of women in advanced positions was weak. Of course, this was in advance of most Arab women.

Historically, Palestinian women were among the first Arab women to take political rights without demanding them and without demonstration.

Bayan Nuwayhed al-Hout

But all testimonies were unanimous in lamenting that women's role in the leadership did not reflect their important role and sacrifices in the struggle.

There are women at the organizational level whose awareness and qualifications are higher than those [men] the PLO has chosen

Amal Masri

This Palestinian leadership did not take the issue of women seriously ... There was no special programme for women, and their representation was not clear or serious in the Revolution's institutions or in the leadership positions.

Amneh Suleiman

Introduction

… there is no woman on the PLO Executive Committee. Even in the wider circles of the PLO the participation of women in advanced positions is weak.

Widad Qomri

The democratic process inside the PLO was not ideal, with dominance and manipulation by Fatah's leadership. Yasser Arafat had the main say in the composition of National Council membership.

Though our representation increased, so did the number of NC members. Abu Ammar, God rest his soul, kept drowning the council with more supporters of the hot issues he was trying to pass by a show of hands.

Mai Sayegh

Abu Ammar brought me back to the Council as an Independent and I joined the Department of Refugee Affairs.

Samira Salah

I became a member of PC when I joined the Executive Bureau of the PRCS, which chose the members with the approval of Abu Ammar.

Hadla Ayoubi

The National Council's 17th Session in Amman was boycotted by some of the factions and by many members in protest at the political agreement between the PLO and the Hashemite Kingdom. Some GUPW members were illegally changed and replaced by a decision of Yasser Arafat, without a meeting of the General Secretariat whose role it was to nominate members. Dropping members needed the consent of two-thirds of the membership.

WOMEN'S LIBERATION/ SOCIAL TRANSFORMATION

The modern Palestinian woman saw women's liberation as essential for her humanity and a pre-requisite for national liberation victory. How much did objective and subjective factors enhance or hinder this aspiration?

No doubt there was a revolution in women's situation, the beginning of real liberation, real social transformation with new revolutionary norms and values, compared to their situation only a few years previously, despite the absence of the social context in the Revolution. Women did not wait to be given their liberation; they grasped it by struggle and determination!

Women were enthusiastic to break their chains, receive recognition, and be integrated into society and the Revolution. People were positive; there were new revolutionary ideas, and great aspirations.

Positive progressive norms were created that replaced the old traditions, and in certain aspects proved stronger than some unimplemented laws. Palestinian women in Lebanon, generally speaking, and many Palestinian women cadres elsewhere, started to represent a new version of women. They were now able to plan their lives, choose their husbands, travel, work, and minimize or drop the dowry. Palestinian society became strongly inclined to enforce its condemnation of polygamy, and any man who married two wives, especially if he were in the Revolution, was usually discredited by both genders. Many Palestinian men changed positively their perception and treatment of women. Though short of complete liberation, these advances became deep rooted in society, mostly among women activists and political cadres.

Though women's issues were not widely discussed, having a say in the politics and tactics of their revolution was a vital part of women's liberation and empowerment.

It was not realistic to expect that major changes in

personal status and civil laws could be made at the time, mainly because of other priorities and the absence of an independent state or a liberated area where the PLO had complete authority; in addition the PLO lacked the social context. Palestinians were expected to adhere to Lebanese laws and the laws of the host countries. A few, including the GUPW, thought that some regulations and laws could have been introduced and implemented at least inside the echelons of the PLO – such laws as forbidding polygamy (though this practice was limited), raising the age of child custody, equal pay for men and women, maternity leave. Such steps were needed to ease women's burdens. They could have limited the occasional anarchy created at times, like enforcing child custody regulations or punishing those who commit the so-called 'honour crime' (though this was a rare phenomenon). The GUPW attempted to have the Personal Status Laws (PSL) legislated for in the 1981 Palestinian National Council session, but the Council could not even find the space to discuss the matter, because of some "important political developments" – the usual excuse for the PLO leadership to close the subject for good.

I think we could have changed laws, especially the personal status laws like polygamy and the custody of children.
Amal Masri

The existence of the Palestinian Revolution affected the social situation in the camp – in both its habits and traditions. Even the most conservative homes were affected by the Revolution's tide.
Fadia Fida

Of course, the Revolution came and gathered a momentum which led to a very big change in our lives as Palestinians ... Women became strong. They would no longer accept oppression.
Amneh Suleiman

In the age of Revolution, female education increased... it also contributed to the improvement of the economic situation of the family and improved girls' marriage conditions ... there were some social services that helped the Palestinians.

Muyassar Ismail

The Palestinian situation in the camps witnessed a big improvement at the economic level and this was reflected by the relatively good standard of living there, though there were serious concerns. Humble houses replaced tin and zinc ones. Lavatories were installed in the houses and the camp abandoned the lavatory blocs that UNRWA had built. The camps were connected to water supplies and medical services were introduced. This improved the situation of the family and especially women.

There was consensus in the GUPW regarding the importance of basic women's rights in general, but there was no real women's movement that expressed comprehensive liberation ideas. The Marxists in the PFLF and DFLP and some in Fateh saw the triple oppression of gender, national and class oppression; others saw the national and gender oppression. A few at that time wanted equality for women but still held to divine laws.

We must reach a state of awareness and democratic dialogue towards a conclusion that would guarantee rights for women – where these rights do not contradict Islamic law or heavenly laws on the land of Palestine.

Intissar al Wazir

Other female leaders who practised their religion were more progressive, asking for a change in laws such as inheritance, divorce and child custody.

Introduction

Women essentially proved their presence by their actions ... but without changing the family status law. However, there must be legislation ...

Issam Abdul Hadi

The Palestinian Revolution elevated the status of Palestinian women at all levels – I can conclude our role was elevated, but remained less than what we had aspired to.

Widad Qomri

We could not fight the women's struggle when we were constantly facing the circumstances of war.

Mai Sayegh

On the subject of the social and the national, and one winning over the other, in that period the national was ahead of the social ... The factions did not make the battle for democracy within the institutions of the PLO, which is the largest platform for the issue of women's democratic rights.

Majida Masri

The PLO realized that women's participation in the struggle was a necessity – after all it was 'A People's War'. However, the National Pact of the PLO did not mention women by name, despite the suggestion to "mobilize all capabilities"; it is as though the cause of equality between men and women was taken for granted.

On the other hand, article 5 of the Pact stresses the patriarchal structure of society, as in most Arab countries; and that a Palestinian was one who lived in Palestine "and all those who are *born to an Arab Palestinian father* after this date inside or outside Palestine", meaning that a Palestinian mother cannot give her children nationality.

However, the PLO's political programme did stress the

33

importance of the promotion of the role of Palestinian women in the national struggle socially, culturally and economically. Support was given to establish the General Union of Palestinian Women, yet in other common fields there was no programme or committee for women.

The absence of a clear social context to the Revolution hindered its development into a full revolution; as did the aggressions of the Israeli/Imperialist/Arab Reactionary forces. The Revolution's ideology was a mixture of liberal conservatism, moderate religiousness, secular nationalism, and Marxism. However, there were no significant differences in practice.

I do not see that either the PLO or any other organization actually worked for the liberation of Palestinian women in the Palestinian Revolution.

Amal Masri

Though the authority of the patriarchal system was weakened, the women's movement never really challenged it. Moreover, there were no special programmes or committees specialized in dealing with direct issues related to legal literacy, violence against women, sexual harassment, or any similar issues. There were workshops and discussions to come out with a paper on family laws that was submitted to the National Council but never discussed there. These problems were discussed inside the women's movement and there was some consciousness-raising around them; the problems were tackled on an individual level by the women's organizations, political organizations, or through family and tribal relations.

There was no system or specialized institution for social and family relations. If advice were necessary it would take place in the framework of whatever organization the fighter belonged to. The solution relied solely on the awareness of the person who was head of that group or organization. There was no centralized authority for family and social relations.

The leadership did not solve sensitive social issues. **Samira Salah** mentions how the GUPW met with PLO leader Abu Ammar and demanded that the perpetrators of the so-called "crime of honour" should be punished. Unfortunately, no action was taken. Though such ugly crimes were rare, the leadership did not tackle them.

Moreover, polygamy still existed on a limited scale; *having more than one wife was not forbidden, but neither was it a social phenomenon.* (Intisar al Wazir)

However, there were some attempts at introducing positive social changes that guaranteed women's rights. **Hadla Ayoubi** said that maternity leave for those working in the Palestinian Red Crescent became 70 paid days, and most Crescent centres had kindergartens.

Kassem Aina affirmed that since Beit Atfal al-Sumoud (BAS) had been established, *men and women employees have held the same rights.*

WOMEN AND MARRIAGE

Palestinian society, like other Arab societies at the time, denigrated unmarried women — if they were poor or did not work, they were often considered a burden on the family. A few cadres chose not to marry. Their response was that of empowered liberated women – there was no stigma in being single.

I have no regrets. ... Just like many female Palestinian activists who really forgot their own lives when their main concern was the cause and its people.
Amneh Suleiman

I never married ... so I say: either a good marriage or no marriage. I didn't feel I had to get married ...
Hadla Ayoubi

GENDER RELATIONS AND WOMEN'S LIBERATION

Social transformation took place in society; it was certainly the result of this long process which changed gender roles and consciousness. Initially most men admired the struggle of the women – as long as she was not their own wife or daughter. There were complexities:

> *'Old habits die hard'. Changing social values and behaviour needs a long time, and it does not happen just by being in a leftist organization.*
>
> **Majida Masri**

This changed with time, even in regard to household duties.

> *The changes I saw in my life between '68 and the 80s were leaps forward.*
>
> **Hasna Rida**

Many men mentioned that their wife had become a partner. Moreover, women started lecturing men cadres about feminism:

> *... Women's struggle and the concept of women's liberation ... I remember that I went to sessions of this sort and spoke about the political and cultural situation regarding women.*
>
> **Shadia Helou**

> *I told the Sheikh that the bond of marriage* was in my bride's hand; .... The experience of the resistance benefited us a lot. We acquired new values which weren't prevalent a long time ago.*
>
> **Kassem Aina**

*both men and women have the same right of divorce

Introduction

Women's Liberation: A New Woman!

I felt I could be at the same intellectual and awareness level as the university girls who were my age. I learned a lot by reading ... I felt my personal independence, everything in me changed.

Hamda Iraqi

My participation opened my eyes to more knowledge, reading and the curiosity to learn. It gave me confidence in myself and in my capabilities.

Fadia Fida

The Revolution is my life ... No, it is certain that the Revolution made deep changes in my life.

Shadia Helou

The truth is that, despite all the disappointments and difficulties, this period represented some of the best days of my life.

Rima Bordcosh

I do not wish that my life were outside the resistance, or that I were not Palestinian.

Basma Antar

Conclusion

This book should help to contribute to bringing the role of Palestinian women out of the shadows, and so it can be recognized on a wider scale. Though the Revolution was halted, all the reasons for a new revolution and Intifada are still there. The Palestinian people are still seeking the most effective method of struggle against their powerful enemies. The struggle has continued in all shapes and sizes inside the Occupied Territory. There was the great

37

Intifada (uprising) in 1987-1991 that was a wonderful mass protest against the Israeli occupation with the wide participation of women. The relentless struggle and sacrifices of our people in the Occupied Territory continues, despite the horrific oppression and long Israeli siege on Gaza and the drastic setback by the signing of the Oslo Accords or the so-called peace agreement in 1993. This agreement is disastrous for all the Palestinian people. From the beginning it offered no guarantee to implement the Palestinians' Inalienable National Rights, mostly the Right of Return of the Palestinian Refugees. On the contrary, it allowed the vast expansion of the Israeli colonialist settlements and persistent ethnic cleansing.

The process of Palestinian women's liberation has begun and there are many irreversible achievements though, unfortunately, it lost its grassroots and popular existence with the end of the Revolution's base in Lebanon. One important achievement, however, was the emergence of a new female cohort composed mainly of women of peasant origin from the refugee camps and petit bourgeoisie. During the Israeli invasion of Lebanon and its aftermath, they were vital in the struggle.

WHERE ARE THESE WOMEN TODAY?

From interviewee profiles we can see how their lives were transformed as they began their road to liberation. They are the New Women – empowered and free to make their personal and political choices. However, as a fact of life, not every woman who participated in the struggle one day kept to this path. Very few of these women cadres opted to support the illusions of the Oslo Peace Agreements and continued to justify the policies of surrender of the Palestinian leadership. On the other hand, the great majority of Palestinian women cadres are struggling with their people against colonial settlers' occupation, racism and ethnic cleansing, opting for the right strategies and means to realise national and women's liberation. They and all the Palestinian people are confident of victory; they know that the democratic state they aspire to build is in sight.

REFERENCES

Justin McCarthy *The Population of Palestine: Population History and Statistics of the Late Ottoman Period and the Mandate* (Columbia University Press – 1990)

David McDowall *Palestine and Israel: The Uprising and Beyond* (I.B. Tauris; New edition – 1990)

Ilan Pappe *The Ethnic Cleansing of Palestine* (Oneworld – 2006)

Rosemary Sayigh *Too Many Enemies* (Zed Books – 1994)

1.

RIMA BORDCOSH

Born to a prosperous and well-educated family who were forced off their lands in the Palestinian seaside town of Jaffa to end up in Lebanon, Rima now lives in Canada. Believing in the power of education and reading to take people along the path to freedom and liberation, in the 1970s she worked tirelessly to establish libraries in the camps in Lebanon. She was responsible for the education committee in the GUPW – Lebanon branch, and became president of the Union there. She later worked as librarian at the Dag Hammarskjold Library of the United Nations until she retired in 2002.

I was born to bourgeois parents in Yafa [Jaffa], Palestine before the Zionist enemy took our homeland in 1948, and the family had no fewer than eight citrus groves with lemon and orange trees, mandarin, and grapefruit, as well as avocado and other produce. In one of the groves off Ajami Street in Yafa, the family owned 'Jaffa Sportive City' where international tennis competitions took place. How beautiful was my mother's voice as she told the story of how she beat the British Commissioner General at tennis and, with my father, won 16 silver cups! My father was an orange trader and a graduate of the American University in Beirut. He would often tell us of the importance of education and study. My mother spoke English and French in addition to Arabic, played the piano, and held the brevet certificate.

In 1948 the Zionist enemy took away our dear land. The whole family was exiled to Lebanon, where life was very difficult – we had lost everything and became refugees. But my parents shared

41

their strong will with all the Palestinian people who were expelled from their land. All the difficulties and poverty we faced did not prevent them from working hard to achieve their first goal: to ensure we were educated at the best Lebanese schools and universities. Eventually I earned a Master's degree in Library Science from Pittsburgh in 1969.

My parents' second important goal was to raise us to love the homeland, Palestine, and to rely on ourselves and be self-sufficient. When the year 1965 came, marking the start of the Palestinian Revolution, I felt the urge to join in.

I went to Pittsburgh University in the American state of Pennsylvania in 1968 to study Library Science. I was surprised by the advanced level of the libraries there, especially the public ones, and their role in developing and advancing society. Why don't we have anything similar? What prevents progress in this field in our country? I decided then that my national duty after graduation would be to contribute to developing and building public libraries in our Palestinian communities. When I returned to Lebanon I joined the General Union of Palestinian Women – Lebanon branch and in 1972 became a member of the cultural committee, whose membership was taken from the different Palestinian organizations. Not long after that, I was elected the committee's president. Yes, it was time for action.

The cultural committee published a yearly programme which included building public libraries in the Palestinian communities with central training facilities for library cadres from all the camps. Beforehand we contacted all the publishing houses in Lebanon, asking them to give us ten copies of every publication. There was a great revolutionary momentum and all kinds of books came to the Women's Union. We were able to collect sufficient books to distribute in the camps and these were used for training purposes. The Palestinian Planning Centre helped bring the cadres from the communities to the Union's centre in Beirut to participate in the sessions.

A public library was established in each camp and after that there were follow-up sessions for every community. Many people joined these libraries and the experience proved that they enjoyed reading. Reading is a good way to instil awareness in women and develop their abilities. But there was some illiteracy among women. The Women's Union decided on a programme to erase illiteracy; training sessions were needed for the cadres to implement it. The Union sought the help of an expert from the Lebanese National Movement and followed the methods of the Brazilian thinker Paulo Freire, who concentrated on the necessity and importance for participants to engage in the adopted political and social processes of their society. Freire's method was based on enabling participants to take control of their lives, which would help them to be free.

The Union held many central and local sessions in the different communities and many women graduated from these literacy classes. The graduation ceremonies were happy and beautiful. What a delight to see women writing letters to their sons in the Fedayeen base. The literacy programme was successful and a major contribution to raising women's awareness, to liberating them, and enabling them to participate in the process of freeing of their land. Unfortunately, the civil war stopped many of these activities. The Union established an educational programme for women which included subjects on national occasions about the Revolution and the history of Palestine, about women's liberation, and raising their children. This programme was implemented at the central and local levels and included all communities. With the Lebanese Civil War, imperial, Zionist, and Arab reactionary attacks on the Revolution and national movement increased. It was my destiny to be elected president of the branch. What a difficult role!

Then came the notorious April 13th 1975, when 23 Palestinians were killed by the Phalangists in Ain al-Rummaneh, as they were returning home to Tal al-Zaatar camp. The resistance and all the unions were mobilized. The Women's Union called for a general meeting to confront the situation. This meeting was a turning point. More than 300 Palestinian and Lebanese sisters came to the Union's headquarters. I told them, 'You are all aware of the dangers the Revolution is going through and we all know who our enemies are. We have to face them with serious work…do not allow anyone to defeat us!' And so we established emergency activities including visiting the wounded in hospital and caring for their needs in coordination with the Palestinian Red Crescent Society, donating blood, and distributing medication in the camps. A committee was formed to take care of the children while mothers were busy volunteering. The next day the Union was filled with new volunteers, the workload increased, and Lebanese women joined with Palestinian women. The Union was the most active of all the unions in the Palestinian arena. The truth is that, despite all the disappointments and difficulties, this period represented some of the best days of my life for then there was hope of reaching our goals.

THE SOCIAL CHANGES

Among the results of women's participation in the resistance were social change and the emergence of new values in women's situation. The concept of women's liberation developed with the growth of women's understanding of the reality they were living through. Women were liberated and they broke the chains that had prevented them from going out of the house as they discovered the freedom of movement to participate in revolutionary work. Women developed their abilities and self-confidence. The Union's role at the level of development of women's social reality was a positive one in their mobilization. Would it have been possible for the PLO to play a bigger role? Yes, it was possible but that did not happen.

In 2008, Rima responded to the questions in writing as she lives in Canada.

Children from Beit Atfal al-Sumoud

2.

FADIA FODA

Now living in Berlin, the mother of three children, Fadia works with refugees and their families, supporting and coaching them with a view to their integration into the labour market. She is a board member of the Ibn Rushd Fund for Freedom of Thought, Berlin. Her family is originally from Akka (Acre) in Palestine. Until 1982 Fadia was a member of Fatah Women's Bureau and responsible for women in Burj al-Brajneh camp. She was also on the executive committee of Popular Aid for Relief and Development as Lebanon director. From 1982 she was a member of the Administrative Committee of the General Union of Palestinian Women – Lebanon branch. In her interview she pays tribute to the work of the GUPW and how it helped develop the lives of so many Palestinian women. She gives a keen insight into the period of the Israeli invasion of Lebanon in 1982 and the important and often unacknowledged role of Palestinian women at that time.

My memories of joining the activities of the Palestinian resistance begin when I was still a schoolgirl about thirteen years old. The camp at that time was the homeland I was looking for. I did not live in the camp or in an area of Palestinian families; my relationship with my identity started the moment I entered Ramallah elementary school in Beirut. At that time the specificity of my identity became clear. I came from a family that was displaced from Acre to the city of Tyre, then to Beirut and finally we settled in Haret Hreik in the southern suburbs of Beirut. In all these places of residence I felt what distinguished the status of my family from the Lebanese families surrounding us. The concerns of my parents and older brothers were clearly different. I remember my eldest brother would stay up at night listening to the radio to follow up on the events in Jordan. As a child I felt that listening to the radio was somewhat of an adventure which might lead to something that would hurt us.

My father is from the Foda family, which is a well-known family in Acre; my mother is from the Kurdi family, also from Acre. As a child I felt proud that my parents were educated and my pride in my mother at the time was clear, especially when I compared her with the mothers of most of my friends and acquaintances. She could read and write Arabic and speak some English. Among the things still carved in my memory is the sight of the upper floor of our neighbours' house where their daughter was being beaten for daring to borrow some books to read, and the sight of the books flying in the air and her father yelling at her and the violence she went through. Why does this stay in my memory? Is it because I had enjoyed the freedom of reading ever since learning the alphabet? This was normal in our house – but not so for many girls; it was still a taboo at the time.

An incident which affected me a lot when I was eight years old and we were still living in Beirut was when my older brother was fired from his job in a metal workshop and deprived of any compensation. I knew early on about discrimination against Palestinian workers. I remember the bitterness my brother felt at the time and my feelings with regard to the injustice he suffered.

At an early age I started to work with the Union of Palestinian Students and I was among the first group to join the Fatah movement within what was called the 'Flowers'. I remember how enthusiastic I was and how I felt the need to move in this direction. Was it my own awareness? No, I don't profess this. It was a matter of enthusiasm and an answer to a question which was worrying me. Who am I and why am I different? I felt that my relationship with the Flowers and my school for refugees was my identity.

Back then all those around us talked about the Fedayeen activities. Burj al-Brajneh camp was where I attended organizational meetings. At the beginning my family did not encourage me or my sister, Faten, who is one year older than me, to do this. My mother would cover our absence and, from time to time, we had to resort to some deception to continue our activity. But, in general, joining the Flowers was overlooked, especially since I benefited from the fact that my cousin, who was a teacher in one of the UNRWA schools, was a Fatah member, and I used this to emphasize the correctness of what I was doing. At that time there was a film about the Palestinian cause in a cinema in Beirut, and the school organized a trip by bus to see it. We watched the film with amazement because it told our story. My classmates and I were very affected by this film. We memorized its details and repeated them to each other many times.

Organizationally, we were followed by a young woman who was a few years older than us. We would meet and she would talk to us and encourage us to read. Once she taught us a little dance which we performed at a school party in the name of the Flowers of Fatah.

The events in Jordan in September 1970 when the PLO and the Jordanian Armed Forces came into conflict, and the uprising of the camps in Lebanon, broke the stagnant situation and induced the whole camp, despite the conservative nature of many of its residents, men and women, to join the resistance. As students, we were at the centre of these events and demonstration was one of our means of expression. Our activities were not always planned, but it was enough for us to hear of a certain event to mobilize all the students in our school to go out into the surrounding streets and chant slogans. This closeness to events motivated me to get to know more.

We would meet at the Women's Union in a two-roomed house in the camp. The library at the Union drew my attention. I was encouraged to borrow books to read.

The first big activity of the Union in which I participated was after clashes with the Lebanese Army in May 1973. The Union organized first-aid training sessions with the co-operation of the Palestinian Red Crescent. It was able to mobilize many women and girls. I interacted well with this session and, afterwards, I participated in voluntary work in a clinic at the entrance to the Burj al-Brajneh camp.

The Palestinian Revolution affected the social situation in the camp – both its habits and traditions. Even the most conservative homes were affected by the Revolution and could not prevent their daughters from contributing to it. Many young women were subject to pressure from their families, but this did not prevent them from challenging their parents and going out to contribute to the activities taking place. The main influence appeared to be on school students.

We started looking to the future and to our role in it. These protests developed awareness in my generation that we could do whatever we thought was right and mobilize our colleagues at school in what we saw as suitable activities. This awareness would not have happened if it were not for the atmosphere that helped it, and for the political and organizational follow-up.

There was no effective role for religion at the time. It was present, but it was not a tool either to allow or forbid any step we made. I do not remember girls and young women of my generation covering their heads. We realized that there were behavioral rules to which we had to adhere. We discussed this from the point of view that respect for beliefs and balanced behavior would earn us the respect of the camp and its residents, which might contribute to the wider participation of women.

The Union's activities at the time included first aid, dialogue seminars, and sessions to abolish illiteracy. These early activities of the Women's Union in Burj al-Brajneh camp were met with great interest and attendance, especially amongst the mothers of girls who were with us in the Union. We discovered that when mothers participated in subjects of interest to them, they felt the importance of what we were doing and gave us more support.

During this period our experience in popular, health and political work advanced quickly. Events required our swift movement. Women's committees were formed to cover voluntary work in local hospitals. Women's military units joined the militias; it was a new experience in the camp to see girls carrying arms and military equipment to participate in armed activities. Other groups of women supplied the fighters with food.

In 1975 we started organizing ourselves. The GUPW and the Fatah Women's Bureau were able to widen our awareness by introducing us to other women's experiences. Once the Union hosted Fatima Ibrahim from Sudan and she told us about the struggles of Sudanese women. We met women from Bahrain and Iraq, and when a delegation from the International Democratic Women's Union visited Lebanon, the Union arranged a tour for them which included the camps, and they had many meetings with the Union's cadres. This was an important opportunity to get to know the common problems relating to women, despite the different circumstances surrounding them. The Women's Bureau started gathering and defining the problems that confronted women in the various camps. This was our first experience of dealing with problems concerning women. The link between national liberation and women's liberation provided the priority in our search for national liberation. This experience helped us open for discussion the specificity of women's situation in our society, which we were working to revolutionize.

We followed up the congresses held in Beirut by the General Union of Palestinian Women, particularly the one convened in 1980. Here we gained new experience by contacting women's delegations from all over the world. I witnessed the problem between the Iraqi Women's League, which was in opposition to the Iraqi regime, and the Iraqi Women's Union, which was pro regime; the latter exerted pressure on the Palestinian leadership to expel the League's delegation from the Congress. This made me wonder how we could be equidistant from the regimes, liberation movements and opposition forces. This question remains.

An experience we lived in detail was preparation for the Union's elections. We had a big campaign in the camps to encourage women to join the Union. This experience was a new opportunity for us to move from the concept of appointments to the principle of elections. We hoped that this mode would turn into a method of work for us in the future, so we could elevate the democratic experience of the Union. Moreover, neither the Palestinian camps nor the women had witnessed before the experience of giving their opinion through elections.

Palestinian women made their contribution within various frameworks of the Revolution, but did they manage to reach decision-making positions? The answer is 'No – I don't think so'. All the potential of women was given to serve our national liberation and to revolutionize and develop the capabilities of Palestinian women. But the work programme was subject to the priorities of the national movement while taking into consideration the status of women.

1982 WAR EXPERIENCE

There were many political lectures warning about the coming Israeli invasion. We heard often from Arafat about the 'accordion' plan in which the Israeli Defense Forces (IDF) and Lebanese Forces would 'squeeze' the PLO. Despite that, we were not prepared at the organizational and political levels for what was coming to us. The Israeli invasion started and we were in chaos the first two days asking ourselves what we should do. When the magnitude of this military operation became clear we started taking initiatives. The first step I took, as the one responsible for Fatah's women's organization in the southern suburbs and in charge of the Beirut area of the GUPW, was to call on all members of the Union and the organizations who had not left the suburbs to meet at a place outside the camp itself, since the camp was being targeted by aircraft in every raid.

To begin with we specified our mission to provide volunteers for the local hospital, which the Palestinian Red Crescent opened in Haret Hreik. At the same time, some women were providing hot meals for the fighters at the fronts. A group of women joined the fighters and they took it upon themselves to give first aid and to fight. This military group of women was in the area of Hayy al-Sillum, controlled by the militia. The group was subjected to heavy bombardment by the Israelis. I worked with Amal Masri, who was also a member of the Union's Beirut leadership, and Suad Hamad also joined us. We formed a team of more than 40 women and had a base and a car to take supplies directly to fighters in the suburbs. Working in such circumstances was not easy. Shelling, destruction and death surrounded us on all sides, but during each period of calm we would resume our work. The International Red Cross representative, who was providing us with supplies, was shocked when she reached our base and the air strikes and bombardment from the sea began. She and her team had to seek protection in the first shelter they found. When the attacks stopped, she discovered that the supplies she had brought had already been moved to the storehouse during the shelling, so she asked us 'where do you get the nerve to endure work under such circumstances?'

One important thing I noticed is that during wars and crises the familial grip over women loosens, which allows us more freedom to take initiatives. Women who had never been part of the Union's work, or members, joined us. They worked with competence and dedication. We took security measures to guarantee the safety of the women who were providing the suburbs' residents with food.

We used flour bags as protection facing the area which we thought might pose a danger to us, as if we knew that they would target our work. Our base was targeted while a group of women were apportioning the supplies. One woman suffered an injury while the rest escaped by a miracle. The driver who was delivering the supplies with us was hit by a direct shell which almost killed him. We lost the car that was transporting us, but we were able to get another one and a driver and we continued in this role.

Through this work we were able to co-ordinate our relations with the different parties in the southern suburbs, the most important of which was the council that emerged from the national movement parties, in addition to members of the social movement. The International Red Cross provided us with necessary supplies for all the southern suburbs and we gave this material to all remaining Lebanese and Palestinian citizens.

In general, this period was one of the most important phases in which we, as women, worked as a single united group. The political and organizational differences disappeared. And here I record much appreciation for the experience of our joint work with Amal Masri from a different organization, working with the utmost dedication within the General Union of Palestinian Women.

NEW VALUES, SOCIAL TRANSFORMATION

No doubt the presence of the Palestinian resistance in Lebanon contributed to certain social changes, especially if we assess the values posed by the resistance in general. The political trends it produced were either national or leftist. They had the principle of national liberation and were open to other experiences in the world. The effect of this on the social situation as a whole can be evaluated by the wide participation of women and young people in the resistance. This period allowed many women to move freely; young women travelled outside Lebanon from all the Palestinian camps for education. I find in this a major social change.

One notices a difference when we see the huge number of female capabilities in the various institutions that the resistance established. This presence forced a change in the social status as there was openness at the level of freedom to choose a partner. Many marriages took place on the basis of free choice made by women. In a few cases where parents didn't accept their daughter's choice, women escaped and made their parents face reality. During all those years no so-called 'honour crime' was committed, and we did not witness any girl being pursued by her parents in this matter. Social compromise occurred and the most conservative people would take the initiative to contribute to it.

There was no issue of multiple wives (polygamy) in the camp. Early marriages were still taking place, but the age was raised to over 16 or 18 years. Many women were engaged to people from the resistance. This was one of the changes because at the beginning the general expression was 'she married a stranger', but with the spread of such marriages this expression disappeared from the camp.

The number of those with higher education increased among young women, which before this was restricted to rich Palestinian families outside the camp.

On a personal level, my participation in the national struggle contributed to the shaping of my character and widening the scope of my thinking. I don't know how I would have been at a personal level if I had not joined this revolutionary atmosphere early on. Sometimes I admit that we are a lucky generation because we had the tools that helped us understand our surroundings and we benefited from this to shape our private and public vision. I feel sorry for the current generation which is lost between the religious streams that are trying to put them back in boxes. My participation opened my eyes to more knowledge, reading and the curiosity to learn. It gave me confidence in myself and in my capabilities. I was able to reach a certain position and get acknowledgement from my family and from the women and men in Burj al-Brajneh camp. It taught me to make choices freely.

As for the general social situation, the Palestinian reality witnessed a big improvement at the economic level and this was reflected by the relatively good standard of living in the camp. Within a short period humble houses replaced tin and zinc ones. Lavatories were installed in the houses and the camp abandoned the group lavatories which UNRWA had built. All these changes would not have been possible if the economic situation had not improved. This was also reflected in nutrition and health levels and extended to the new social values that the camp began to accept.

However, the resistance could have done more to improve the brutal situation in the camp; the open sewers did not disappear in Burj al-Brajneh and, at the time of writing, the camp still gets rid of this water in pits awaiting a suitable time to be emptied. Despite the passage of all these years the resistance, with all its capabilities, could not solve this dangerous health issue; nor did UNRWA.

The dowry system was no longer an obstacle to marriage. The agreement of both parties was essential. A woman's beauty was not the only thing sought, but also her education. As for pregnancy and having [many] children, it is evident that the new generation abandoned such practice and this was considered to reflect further social awareness.

The camp lived with a limited number of 'prostitutes' or women with a bad reputation. The young men in the camp knew the address to go to for their sexual needs. But talking about it was always in a low voice. The area where these women lived was called Al-Batiniyya. Such behaviour was overlooked, and no one confronted these cases.

The PLO could have played a major role in support of the equality of women and their liberation, but I think they did not give this aspect enough attention. They were satisfied with representing women as one of the shapes in the picture and not out of conviction for the importance of women's role. They did not offer an example of equal participation, and if we look at the representation in different frameworks, from the national council to the executive committee, we will discover the actual numbers of women they wanted in the ranks of the PLO. It was possible to elevate the participation of women and their representation. Yet, despite all the pressure exerted by female cadres, they could not increase the representation. I don't think the PLO had the programme or the will for this. But I value the roles the PLO made women participate in and appreciate the allocation of places for educational and career qualifications in the socialist countries. The credit here goes to the Women's Union, which allocated those places.

The PLO and its institutions, and the resistance, played a role in freeing women economically. No doubt full-time employment in the different frameworks of the PLO and the resistance in general freed women from being financially dependent, which imposed a new reality on the family. I am among those women who owe their rich experience to the General Union of Palestinian Women, and to contact with the General Secretariat. The Union tried through its activities to develop the local female cadres who had no previous experience in this domain, and it was able to reach every camp and shape the units of female work there. When I look back at the beginnings of our work, the female cadres who represented women centrally had the task of moving from one camp to the other and had several roles, until local frameworks, after a short period, were able to assume their role.

The Union's activities contributed to taking women out of their shells and opening new horizons for them to develop their awareness. At times of danger its cadres would be in the front line in all domains.

Fadia Foda sent written answers to the interviewer's questions. December 2007

3.
SHADIA HELOU

Originally from Nazareth, Shadia's family became exiled to Lebanon where Shadia herself was born. The trigger for her political involvement was the battle of Karameh and the 1967 defeat. For many Palestinians, education was the goal to aim for, and Shadia's parents were no different in their desire for their children to have the best education possible. But neither did they stand in the way of their involvement in the national struggle. Shadia's education served her well and she found work in journalism, translating and writing. From 1977 to 1982 she was responsible for the organization of women in Fatah-Lebanon, and in the same period was president of the GUPW's Lebanon branch. From 1993 to 2008 she worked in the office of the President of the National Authority, Yasser Arafat, media and women section, and was a member of the Palestinian National Council.

Shadia talks about the massacre of inhabitants of Tal al-Zaatar and the siege, and about military training for women and their participation in battle areas. Of the GUPW she points to the fact that some of their projects needed to be self-supporting due to the lack of funds, and how the women of different factions came together to ensure those projects went forward. Women's equality was a huge issue, as was further education, with the socialist bloc offering training in the medical professions and engineering. Apart from an education of the more conventional kind, Shadia sees the Revolution itself as having opened up a whole different world to her, from culture to philosophy, from religion to sociology – an otherwise unexplored life.

I grew up in an uprooted Palestinian family and we always lived the Palestinian cause. My family was uprooted from Haifa in Palestine and I was born in Lebanon. At the beginning I used to hear about the struggle and the revolution, but the real start was after the battle of Karameh. I was very aware of the terrible defeat of 1967. There was a new awareness regarding the Palestinian-Israeli conflict and as I started to hear more about Fatah, I became enthusiastic to join this movement and contribute to the fight for the liberation of Palestine.

Of course in the family the nationalistic atmosphere was always present and regaining our country was everyone's goal. My father's experience was mainly in the labour movement in Palestine. My parents' main concern was for us to be well educated, i.e. not lower than university level. The first years of the uprooting were very hard, especially since we were six girls in the family.

I joined the Palestinian national liberation movement in 1968 and my sister Jehan is the one who drafted me – in the kitchen!! The activity was secret.

My father was not keen on parties and organizations, maybe because of the spirit of defeat after the Nakba. The people had their doubts about the effectiveness of the armed struggle at its beginning, especially the older generation. "Where will this lead?" they would say. But when they saw this Palestinian movement growing, they were happy that their children were participating, while at the same time fearing for them.

But honestly, to say a word for history, our parents did not prevent us from participating in the struggle at all, despite everything. Sometimes they tried to decrease our momentum. When I was working in more than one domain I remember my father telling me not to carry a thousand watermelons at one time, so that I would concentrate on less and have better results.

I started working with students – though I might have chosen another domain, possibly in the media. Frankly speaking, when I worked with women it was because I felt the necessity to work with them and not because I loved this work, which is very tiring. I felt that as an educated person I had a duty towards Palestinian women to help them strengthen their position in order to participate in the Palestinian struggle.

MY WORK WITH WOMEN

Discrimination against women is present in the very marrow of our society. It is present among women and men, mainly because it is a masculine society – women were raised to be against themselves and to know that they are subordinate in society.

I worked initially in Tal al-Zaatar, but as president of the Women's Union Lebanese Branch I had dealings with all the camps in Lebanon. There were still restrictions on women. People were religious but not fanatical and, of course, there were difficulties in working in the camp.

I started organizing in Tal al-Zaatar in 1975. Most of its population, men and women, were workers, because it was close to the Lebanese industrial area. Because the women were doing their jobs all day I could only see them at night, which required me to sleep in the camp and that created a problem with my parents. This was at the beginning of '75 before the Lebanese civil war. I would give the excuse that I was sleeping at my married sister's place. This was a major experience for me, new and special, at a time when people were being slaughtered according to their identity (ethnicity and religion). I was known to be a Christian and working in the camp, which was mainly Muslim; this shows how the Palestinian people had completely overcome the sectarianism issue – they made no distinction between Muslims and Christians. National identity and the national challenge are more important for the Palestinians. We should not forget of course that the Phalangist and Lebanese forces did not spare the Palestinian Christians and the Lebanese Christians who were opposed to their scheme.

The Conflict was Political with a Sectarian Face

I worked indirectly when communicating with the working women in the camp. It was important to open avenues for discussion, so I used popular proverbs. We would say a popular proverb, explain it and talk about the political situation. However, this work did not last long because on 13th April 1975 Tal al-Zaatar camp fell victim to an attack by the Phalangist on a bus carrying civilians. I lived the tragedy of the people who were killed and whose families were massacred there. Following that event there was much tension in Tal al-Zaatar camp and work was very difficult because it was under siege in1976. I had to stay there for long periods, until the camp finally fell. I came to know a major part of the camp. There was cooperation between the sisters and the fighters. The siege of Tal al-Zaatar lasted for about 76 days. Women played a major role as nurses in caring for the injured and in guarding the camp, as they had military training. They would provide food and basic needs for the camp, which was bombed continuously, and for the fighters who were defending the camp's borders. Work in Tal el Zaatar was very dangerous. I had to pass through zones where there were kidnappings and snipers and was in danger more than once – I am alive by mere chance!

The attack on the bus of inhabitants from Tal-al Zaatar triggered the spark of the civil war in Lebanon. I was out of Beirut at the time on an organizational mission in the north. I came back to find everything closed. The Arab university area was crowded with angry people and those who felt the enormity of what had happened, but not knowing what to do exactly. I was asked to drive over to the eastern suburbs of Beirut and explore the area as I knew it well; it was very scary. When I got there I found the streets completely empty; there were armed people hiding in buildings. I went back and gave my report.

THE MASSACRE OF TAL AL-ZAATAR

The fall of Tal al-Zaatar and the massacre was a huge tragedy – a real genocide took place. There were barbarous killings. When the inhabitants were evicted from the camp they were in very bad shape. It was a new disaster. There had been a plan of ethnic cleansing. I remember a short time before the attack one of our officers had warned us about it. We had laughed at him saying it was impossible that the Phalangist Lebanese forces would attack the camp – it was too far-fetched. But it happened!

When the camp fell and the people were displaced, they were taken to Damour. I was among the first to receive them. We as a revolution did not prepare for this emergency quickly enough, although we had had experience of this type of situation. Sometimes you would feel it was like resurrection day because of the chaos. As days went by the situation calmed down but remained difficult. Some had lost their mother or father or sibling(s) and some did not know what had happened to members of their families; there were not many men, and the situation was tragic, but there was no real plan about what to do.

I personally was devastated by the fall of Tal al-Zaatar as I had known and shared experiences with the inhabitants there, and I was moved by the way they were treated after the fall of the camp. We proved once more that we had failed in how to help our people with all our capabilities quickly and in an orderly manner.

MILITARY TRAINING

All men and women in the organization had to have military training. This was established in Fatah. I personally had more than one training session and led more than one military camp where training and political education took place. Fatah embraced the armed struggle. Defending the Revolution and its presence in

Lebanon was paramount in order for the resistance to prove itself and be able to fight the Zionist enemy. So the Palestinians were busy organizing themselves inside the camps.

There was a role for women in giving first aid. First aid posts were established in hot areas and mobilization took place in residential areas. Only a few women went to fight elsewhere, such as in the hotels area, where there was heavy fighting. Because it was considered a strategic area it was destroyed, resulting in many martyrs. Some women participated in the front lines in Shiyah.

There were many military training camps for women in Fatah; political education was also given, and criticism and self-criticism practised. This was taken seriously. Lecturers came from outside the camp, and women participants also gave lectures.

Two training camps took place in Beirut. One was during bombing by the hostile right-wing Lebanese forces on the nationalist areas. Though many bombs fell around Bir Hassan camp, the girls were able to complete the training. The majority of them were able to sleep in the camp, though some would go home and come back in the early morning.

In the second camp Israeli airplanes bombed again less than one aerial kilometer away from us. They also bombed Burj al-Brajneh when we were nearby. The planes were low and terrifying. But we were more prepared and most of the girls ran to a nearby building; however, some of them could not run, and if the airplanes had bombed us there would have been huge losses. We discovered later that there had been an operation, and there was concern that the Israelis would respond by bombing us in Lebanon; everyone, but us, had been told to evacuate. We considered this omission to be a big issue. We tried to investigate and to hold those responsible accountable – but of course there were no results.

The third camp was in the South. They also had military training and political education. We brought the daily newspapers to the camp to train the girls to follow up on daily politics. We stayed there only three days because it was bombed for an hour and a quarter by F16 Israeli airplanes. By pure coincidence all the girls were hidden among the trees and we were told not to move because any movement would indicate our positions. I stayed for an hour unable to move because I was in a visible area, but in the end when I saw that the bombing was all on one place, I moved in the last quarter of an hour in the opposite direction. One sister had a minor injury – a stone hit her face from the bombing – and nothing happened to the rest. We were in the valley, and then we went up the mountain, pulling out like an organized army. Our belongings were lost in the tents but everyone got their hats and put them on their heads and left. There was no panic in a situation where women might be thought to be afraid, and a hundred girls pulled out of the valley in an honourable manner.

Of course as women we used to participate in the military parade on the anniversary of the revolution. There were some suggestions from Abu Ammar about establishing a women's military division, and he suggested having women guards. We did not agree to this, as we felt that it wasn't a serious suggestion – women should not just be for decoration.

GUPW GRASSROOTS BASIS & ACTIVITIES

It took great efforts to build the organizational structure of the GUPW in Lebanon; we had committees in all areas where Palestinians lived, and as our base became wider the Union blossomed, though there were some barriers. The biggest of these was that the Union was working with only sporadic financial support and there was no specific budget. The PLO supported the salaries of the teachers of the kindergartens, the nursery and the kitchen team, and provided the food.

The Union had some activities other than childcare which decreased the burden on women. There was the cafeteria in a central location where at least 40 people would come daily to have lunch for a token price. Then we had a limited income through central activities; there was more than one exhibition of handicrafts from all areas. The cadre was made up mostly of women in their twenties and thirties. But housewives too benefited a lot from the activities such as health sessions, first aid and civil defence and literacy programmes. Most of the participants were housewives in the camp.

We all put an effort into promoting national unity inside the GUPW. All those who worked in the Union from the different Palestinian organizations benefited a lot; there was a decrease in organizational fanaticism.

KINDERGARTENS

With the cooperation of the GUPW General Secretariat the experience of the kindergartens was distinguished. We trained teachers and coordinated with international institutions, mainly UNICEF, who supported us; there was continuous training to improve the qualifications of the kindergarten teachers all the way from the north to the south in all our camps, where we had at least 17 kindergartens. Thus the female cadres would exchange experiences and develop their values, vision and the curriculum for the kindergartens.

Then we had a major experience in 1978 when the south was invaded. Many people were displaced. There was a huge mobilization and we decided that the sisters would go to the south and stay there to help settle the people, dig trenches and help people return to their homes

Shadia Helou

INTERNATIONAL WOMEN'S DAY

There was a big development in our activities, especially after the Union proved itself. We had some central activities, the most important of which was on 8th March, International Women's Day. We used to have celebrations in all the camps with the participation of the popular committees and organizations and a central celebration in Beirut. Abu Ammar, George Habash [PFLP] and Nayef Hawatmeh [DFLP] would come to the GUPW-General Secretariat and talk about the important role of women in the struggle. In the last few years there were celebrations in every camp. I consider that this celebration had worth to a great extent because new values were being put forward and discussed.

We concentrated a lot on the cultural aspect. Let us say that there was more individual initiative than organizational initiative. When Abu Omar (Hanna Mikhail) became in charge of the Women's Bureau we set up a cultural programme that continued. This was most important. In general at that time most people were able to read. Many of the cadres would read and learn more.

We as a women's union wanted to work. What were our views on women's issues? What was our role? When we raised the slogan of equality, in what aspect did we want it? Why equality? We talked of "men and women together" and issues of that sort. You have to give content to each slogan by itself with the why and the how. There were talks about the experiences of other peoples, of course in a progressive manner. Certain books or subjects came up for discussion. What were the problems that women were suffering from? When we, of the Fatah women's office, held half-monthly meetings, this was very positive. We used to ask the girls to sleep over at the centre and speak of their experiences and issues of concern whether organizational or personal. Many times we would end the night with songs and dancing, and I must mention here that we took the decision to dance because there was a taboo in that period on dancing, that the girls freed themselves from – I myself learned to dance then. The posing of social issues was on a one-to-one level at the beginning then with the group. Similar activities took place with the women's union too.

PALESTINIAN WOMEN IN VIETNAM

Women cadres from the GUPW went to Vietnam in 1980 to study the experience of women there. Of course we benefited from that experience. I personally was interested enough to translate a book about Vietnamese women. There were always attempts to study such experiences.

INTERNATIONAL SUPPORT

In Tal al-Zaatar many girls attended the first session to study nursing in the Soviet Union in 1973. Many people went, although the official responsible for the district initially had his doubts as to whether the parents would agree.

Among the gains of the Palestinian Revolution was the international support at the time, the support it got from the socialist bloc. Hundreds of Palestinian girls from Lebanon, the Occupied Territory, and Jordan went to the socialist countries for their education. This was very positive because doctors, engineers and specialists graduated from there. This had a positive effect, made by the Revolution in the lives of Palestinian women; before, girls had not been allowed to travel and leave their parents.

WOMEN'S LIBERATION

Men in general, the cadres for sure, could see the developments in women's liberation. Let us not forget the effect of an operation lead by Dalal al-Mughrabi in 1978 – a heroic operation [inside the

Green line] acknowledged by the Revolution, in favour of women. This was also accompanied by the brave participation of women in the Revolution and in heroic operations in the Occupied Territory resulting in many women martyrs and detainees.

All this left a great impact on the collective sentiments of the Palestinian people in general and of the revolutionaries in particular. When there were educational sessions for the organization they would invite the sisters to speak; mostly they would talk of women's struggle and the concept of women's liberation, but in some cases they would invite us to talk on other topics. I remember that I went to sessions of this sort and spoke about the political and cultural situation regarding women. The main struggle was to defend the Revolution personified by the people, so there was more general talk of women's liberation and that women should participate in the same way as men; but there was no specific view regarding the subject of women in a social context. Of course there were some leftist organizations such as the Popular Front and the Democratic Front, that would pose these issues in their social intercourse, but in practice, regarding women and their participation in decision-making inside the organizations and in practice, they were hardly different from Fatah.

In the absence of vision there was some chaos. Let us say that people were positive rather than negative because there were new ideas, revolutionary ideas, there was a dream. But on the other hand it is true that there were wrong practices, although to begin with the general attitude was positive, and we had freedom in women's work and initiatives and could work without coming up against certain red lines.

There were new slogans in the Palestinian arena such as: "Women and men together to liberate Palestine", "My honour is my land". The Revolution progressed in phases. You do not have a productive society to begin with. You are a refugee with no rights and no status and no legal framework that protects you whereby you can pose matters. This was not available on the Lebanese stage in this sense, and there was no legal framework of a state. The most important thing was to work on abolishing illiteracy: and then abolishing cultural illiteracy. We cared very much about establishing the tradition of reading. We built libraries in all the camps. We established classes for abolishing illiteracy and had qualified teachers to give these sessions. We used books for studying, not just books at random. There was always someone to give a lecture. We also made opportunities for self-education. The cadres themselves had to take a subject and many times it would be about women's issues.

The Palestinian people did not have a women's movement that expressed clear liberation ideas. There was no social content and it was difficult to have one. But we wanted to make way for the abilities of the Palestinian people, including women.

The Lebanese experience lasted 12 years practically, but it was not seen through. Social change takes time; even if you make progressive laws, habits and traditions are stronger than laws, and this experience was aborted. Because we do not have a state, there are no legal references or laws that govern us, and most of the Palestinian Revolution's time in Lebanon was spent in battle. You do not think alone, the main party did not think, your main organization did not think, and you as a women's movement are required to think, but this needs relative calm, which was not available.

The Revolution is my life. I became aware with the revolution and developed with it. Before it I didn't know where I was. It opened up a whole new world, a world related to politics, sociology, philosophy and religion. All my culture was turned upside down. Before I was an ordinary Palestinian girl wandering, I was still young. No, it is certain that the Revolution made deep changes in my life.

The interview took place in Ramallah in two sessions in October and December 2007.

*Yasser Arafat welcoming the president of the
Women's International Democratic Federation*

4.

HAMDA IRAQI

Hamda is a Palestinian who was able to return following the Oslo Agreement. She now lives in Nablus after years of exile in a refugee camp in Lebanon with her family, who came from Nakhle al-Nusf, a district of Acre. She lived the various stages of the Palestinian struggle in the camp, firstly under the repressive fist of the Lebanese Deuxieme Bureau state security, then through the growth of the resistance movement, the long siege of the Palestinian camp of Tal al-Zaatar, the Israeli invasion of Lebanon in 1982, and the massacre of Sabra-Shatila. Her commitment to the revolution led her to train in electronics and communications and she became a colonel in Fatah's wireless department. She was a member of the General Union of Palestinian Women and of Fatah.

My family is originally from a town in Palestine between Haifa and Akka [Acre] called Nakhle al-Nusf. Today it is inhabited by Russian Jews and they call it Kiryat Motzkin.

My family was uprooted in 1948. They had problems with the British over the land. The Zionist occupation expelled us. My parents suffered a lot to reach south Lebanon when I was barely a few months old. I grew up knowing that we were living as exiles in Beirut. Around 1965 we were forced to go to Tal al-Zaatar camp – we were 13 or 15 families, all relatives.

It was difficult to build in the camp. We built two small rooms with a zinc ceiling. Bullets would easily penetrate it and, in winter, we couldn't hear each other for the sound of the rain on the roof. In summer it was hot and cold in winter. We were six girls and two boys. My father's worry was to feed us. The only work available was picking oranges.

I studied in the United Nations Relief and Works Agency (UNRWA) school in the Nahr area until the sixth elementary grade, and continued my middle school in Sin al-Fil until the 'Brevet' certificate. UNRWA had only two classes after the sixth grade: seventh and eighth. I wanted to enrol in a secondary school but things were difficult, so I started work at the Ghandour biscuit factory.

The situation of women in the camp was difficult. Some families did not allow girls to go out; older women would work in the flower gardens nearby. The younger women could work at the Ghandour factory or as maids. We were able to go out alone – because my father had grown up as an orphan, he didn't like to upset his daughters. He used to say, 'It's alright to upset the boys, but not the girls'.

The 'Deuxième Bureau' [Lebanese Intelligence Service] was very repressive. For example, if we wanted to hammer in a nail or build something we had to get the agreement of the 'Deuxième Bureau'; we had to bribe them. If someone was troublesome, they would confine him for a month and then let him out so that he would cause further trouble. That way people would go on paying.

I joined the resistance movement when the Palestinian Liberation Army held training sessions and there were girls training, too. From the window of our house which was near the training camp we would watch the girls in their military uniform and wanted to join in, but we were afraid to ask. My cousin was always telling us to join, so we enrolled. We bought our military uniforms for five liras and started training. We remained in the organization for a long time – without the knowledge of our parents. We participated in social affairs and with the families of martyrs.

Hamda Iraqi

JOINING THE WIRELESS SYSTEM

In 1975, I worked at Samed [Palestinian economic institution] in Fakhani, a Beirut neighbourhood close to Shatila camp, in the sewing division. Then there were training sessions in using the wireless. The organization nominated me for training. Those who came top were selected to work in Central Operations, so I left Samed and joined Operations.

The first ones in the section were Sajida Dughman, Nadia Abu Issa and me. Nadia was killed in 1982, while working in the wireless section in the Sanayeh building during an Israeli air raid. Almost all the girls working in the section had finished university. I was the least educated and afraid to fail. I had not studied as much as they had, but I was addicted to reading, and things went well. There was a girl who was as educated as me, but she became afraid and left. I didn't like them saying that she couldn't cope because she was a girl.

Communications with the camp were cut off when the main siege of Tal al-Zaatar began. A group of young men came to take arms from the operations unit. I asked permission of Abu al-Walid, God rest his soul, to go to Tal al-Zaatar. He refused at first, but later accepted when I insisted. He gave me some clippers for cutting the barbed wire and some other things, including a book which he said was mine to keep.

We went by car to Aley where we stayed for three days. A large amount of arms were stored there, still immersed in grease. We would boil water in big pots and pour it over the arms to melt the grease. I cooked for the men — there were no dishes. We then entered a Kuwaiti mansion in Aley where one bed was big enough to sleep four people. I made salad and we made a cone with the cover of *Palestine the Revolution* magazine, like they do in the market, and ate from it. We walked at night from Abadiyyeh to Tal al-Zaatar. We were sixteen people, the guide, and me. I was the only girl. As we were walking, I felt as if something was preventing

75

me from lifting my foot. The men were carrying a lot of arms. I was carrying the wireless set weighing 7 kilograms and its battery, maybe 2 kilos, as well as my personal weapon. I was afraid I wouldn't be able to keep up with the young men, so they made me walk with the guide, with all of them behind me. Sometimes there were houses below; we would go up to avoid them. Once they all shared one cigarette, shielding it with their hands for the light not to show. Another time the guide discovered that we were going the wrong way, so we had to go back. The guide was the master of the road.

We got to a point where I heard young men from the camp calling, 'who is there?' All of them were at the ready. I said, 'no one asks "who is there" except *our own* men'. When they approached, I was afraid that they might not be our men. But then I heard kisses being exchanged. I arrived home at sunrise. There was a dog nearby. The house was gone, it had been burnt down. My parents were inside an iron factory, and the dog would not allow anyone to enter. My father couldn't open the door at first, and my mother shouted 'who did you come with? You've put the family to shame, everyone is talking about you! I wish I had six children instead of you. You spent the whole night with sixteen men?'

She talked on and on but, in the end, she heated the water and they all bathed. We made our first [wireless] connection with appliances and aerial systems. I received a personal cable from Abu Ammar saying 'we congratulate you on arriving safely. May God be with you ...' It stayed in my pocket till the last day. When I walked through the camp, both those who knew me and those who didn't would call 'hi'. One young man asked for my hand in marriage and my father told him, 'this is a man, she needs a man!' The Lebanese Forces [right-wing Christian militia of Bashir Gemayel] would slaughter young men and when we saw a young man over fourteen we would congratulate him. I became very popular in the camp, everyone wanted to talk.

We took a room and set up the apparatus on the roof, which had been all but destroyed. Adham was just saying that the bombardment was coming from there, so immediately I grabbed the apparatus and hung on to it. The first strike hit the cable which transfers current from the electrical system to the battery to recharge, so now I had to take the apparatus with the battery to somewhere I could charge it — there was no longer a charger because it had been hit. I would carry the apparatus with its battery and go to the mosque, wait until it was charged and then bring it back. The mosque was at the end of the road. I only saw my parents every six days; day and night became one.

This continued for a while, then they told me to sleep during the day. But I couldn't sleep because the wireless room was also the leadership room, the meetings room and everything was in it.

The wounded in the mosque suffered increasingly from worms and gangrene. One of them would grab his leg, and when he pressed it the worms would emerge. Imagine someone living with worms in his body; the worms reached a stage beyond prayer. They would remove them with zinc boards. A shell hit the place where there was a hole like a mass grave and the dead bodies flew about near the mosque, which was the Red Crescent centre. No one was able to be buried. I had a sister who was struck in the head; they buried her in the shelter where my parents were. People were buried in any empty space. Even today my mother says my sister's hand was visible, that they didn't bury her well. A shell had hit the staircase when she and my mother were closing the door. A mortar exploded over them hitting my mum's hand – to this day there are splinters in it. My sister was hit in the head and died instantly. She was 12 years old.

On the last day before leaving I burnt all my papers and went to the wireless office. I sprayed the keys, removed the pin from my weapon and threw it.

The day the camp fell was terrible. I put my clothes on and carried a little child; my mother was holding on to me at the Fundukieh (hotel management school) in Dikwaneh, banging her head against the ground and cursing. We left in trucks. Any child aged ten and above would be kicked by the Lebanese Forces, who with their guns pushed people out of the truck onto the ground. A three-year-old girl was killed when she was trampled on. One of the Lebanese militia lifted her by her hair and put her on a donkey. My mother and father, my remaining brother and I reached the museum crossing-point by car with great effort.

When we reached the museum we were thirsty. There were security forces there with the green hats, the Deterrent Forces [Arab League intervention force] and they told us to go straight ahead. There were cars at Bir Hassan waiting to take the people who came from the camp: cars of the armed struggle. However, we didn't go with them; we went to my uncle's house. After Tal al-Zaatar we went for a while to Qassimiyyeh and then to Damour.

During the siege of Beirut I was working in the central operations section in Fakhani. With the first Israeli air strike the two floors above were gone and we moved to the Engineering College. We entered the college through the back door, stayed for a while there, but then we were bombarded again. They were targeting ground floors and air raid shelters. We moved from the Engineering College – there were always alternative operations. The one who comes out alive from one place would go to another … We went from the Engineering College to Burj Abu Haidar …

I remember the shelter there was fewer than three or four steps of iron and cement. The shelling penetrated this fort and broke the iron stairs. Abu Aala's driver, who was with us at the time, was wounded. All the people in the building came down to the shelter with us when the shelling started. When it receded somewhat the people ran away, but when the bombardment from the air continued, we couldn't leave. As the shelling became a little less again, Abu Moussa, one of the military leaders, told us now was the time to leave. We said, 'when you go, so will we'. 'Go out!' he yelled, and so we left. He told us each to go in a different direction. The next morning, we went to Ras al-Nabah, to the shelter of a building that was still under construction. Its shelter was very poor and it also was hit.

We moved to two or three buildings in Ras al-Nabeh. I was allergic to the smell of paint and cement which was terrible, two floors underground. Even the Bic pen wouldn't write, due to high humidity. Then we went to Hamra. When we arrived I told Ussama I hadn't passed by Nadia that day. Her voice had sounded sad and I felt she might have a problem, so I asked him to let someone relieve me while I went to see her. Ussama said 'Ok, there is some fresh meat, can you cook it for the boys first – they haven't eaten for a long time'. I cooked the meat and waited while they had lunch. Abu Hassan was still washing his hands when there was the sound of a bomb. Poor Nadia! She was killed by that bomb. We waited for the dust to settle and then her mother identified her from the tip of her foot and the earrings she was wearing. Many people were killed by this vacuum bomb.

Abu Ammar never stayed with us for long – he would come and go. He became like an infected person! Whenever he entered a building people would run away, because any building he was known to be in was shelled. We met at the port during the departure from Lebanon.

When our fighters left Beirut, Lebanese people sprinkled them with rice – too much rice; it created a rice crisis!

My brother Mustapha left Lebanon with the last group of Palestinians to leave. I told him, 'I thought you weren't leaving'; he replied, 'Didn't you hear that man Bashir swearing and threatening what he would do to those Palestinians who remained in Lebanon!' [Bashir Gemayel of the right-wing Phalangist party, elected Lebanese President in 1982 under the Israeli invasion and assassinated in September.] My brother went to Tartous on the northern coast of Syria and from there he came back to the Bekaa. The night of Bashir's assassination, I slept in Rawsheh, in a building where there were refugees from Dbayyeh camp. I didn't leave, I stayed; but how could I stay? I would go in the morning, not knowing that when the Israeli army tanks came to search the area, I would stay with Deebe, my sister, who worked in the hospital.

I had stayed to see my parents and provide them with a home. Tal al-Zaatar was gone. I was in Fakhani when the massacre of Sabra and Shatila took place. That same day I met a girl at Dana, the entrance to Sabra. She told me: 'They put my mother and brother against the wall and killed them in front of me'. When I told people they would say, 'Don't spread rumours'; they didn't believe me. But after three days it became public. My mother would go down daily with the civil defense and help to identify the dead bodies. She knew many people in the camp. In the end, those who were unidentified were taken to an area near the Kuwaiti embassy and buried in a mass grave.

I had no job. I left Beirut in 1983 and went to Tunisia to where my fiancé and his group had been evacuated, but I was unable to work until they started a branch for the General Union of Palestinian Women there. By then I had given birth to Tarek. There is a year and a month between Tarek and Ala'.

THE REVOLUTION CHANGED MY PERSONALITY

Despite my lack of formal higher education, I felt I could be at the same intellectual and awareness level as the university girls who were my age. I learned a lot by reading. Fatah – not school – taught me to read books and summarize them. I felt my personal independence, everything in me changed. I wouldn't have this awareness if I hadn't joined Fatah and participated in group work.

I prefer group and women union work to organizational work – when you are dealing with people who think differently from you, you benefit more.

MARRIAGE

In 1981, when I returned from Bulgaria where I had been for cadre training with a group of Palestinians, I found my future husband visiting my parents; he knew them and had heard of me. Everything indicated that he was a good person. I got to know him before marriage; he would visit my parents and we could sit together alone at home. He used to borrow books from me. I had a library at home in Damour. My mother used to criticize me: 'Look at other girls — they buy gold but you buy paper'. I would always buy books from exhibitions in Beirut and my brother made me wooden shelves for them.

My husband read too. He treated me with respect. In Tunisia our situation was very good because I was connected to the GUPW. But when we went to Baghdad the environment was different. The people we knew there were from the Baath party and the Arab Front. They married in the traditional manner. My husband did not want anyone to know that I had travelled back and forth.

When we returned to Palestine after the Oslo Agreement there was disappointment with the general situation. On a personal level, my husband re-married. He worked with the Palestinian Authority.

Looking back now at the Tal al-Zaatar massacre, I would say that the sufferings of the people there did not get the attention they deserved. They suffered a lot, but their experience was not known widely enough to benefit from it; in its spontaneity everyone in the camp participated in the struggle and remained steadfast.

We used to blame the leadership when we were in the camp but when we left, many who used to say 'Forget the phase of Amman' [when the Palestinians were evicted from there to Beirut], started then to say 'Forget Tal al-Zaatar', and they now tell you 'Forget Beirut', as if there is no connection between them. Over here [the West Bank], I would hear in the Nablus area that Beirut is gone, 'Do not talk of Beirut'. Beirut may be gone, but I am a daughter of Fatah of the Revolution: Fatah is not gone. We do not know our history.

If I were to make choices for my life again, I would choose the same path of resistance. I made no mistakes and I regret nothing – I was convinced of all I did.

International Women's Day

5.

MUYASSAR ISMAIL

Coming from a peasant Nazarene family living in exile in Burj al-Shimali camp in Lebanon, Muyassar describes what life was like there for families of similar background. She gives a general picture of the infrastructure of the camp and of the work that was acceptable for women to do to eke a living for their families. From the village of Malaloul in Palestine, via a camp in Lebanon, she ended up in Amman, Jordan, on the way following a career as a social worker, eventually becoming director of the Guesthouse of the Child and Family Guidance/Jordan Women's Union. From 1978 to 1983 she was secretary of Fatah Women's Office in Tyre, Lebanon, and of its office for Lebanon as a whole. In the same period she was a member of the Administrative Committee of the GUPW Lebanese branch. In Jordan she became Central Council Member of the Jordanian Women's Union. Among other things her interview covers changes in religious practice, and changing relations between men and women.

I grew up in Burj al-Shimali camp, Lebanon, in a poor family of 12. My father was a construction worker and up until the preparatory level I studied in the UNRWA schools. I stopped studying for a while due to the economic situation and the arrival of the resistance movement in Lebanon, though I resumed my studies later.

My ambitions at first were limited to studying, marriage, and having a family and children. But with the Revolution my goal changed; it became bigger and nobler, that is, to be involved in politics. This was in the early 1970s when active work became almost public. I was careful to keep it secret and not speak of any of the activities even to those closest to me. I faced difficulties at

85

the beginning, as my father feared the effect of my going out and becoming involved in politics, for the social context surrounding us in general did not allow for girls to be involved in such matters or even in ordinary work. Gradually, and with time, the situation got better regarding freedom of movement, because I proved myself on the ground and did not damage my parents' reputation; on the contrary, there was mutual trust between us, even with neighbours and friends.

There was a big and double burden on me because of this involvement. I had to do all my duties at home before attending any outside activity so that my mother would not feel the Revolution to be a burden on her or that it took me away from her, and for my father I kept the social traditions of the camp. So I won the respect and love of my parents, and they accepted my situation. My situation improved as the Revolution, with its armed presence, became public. It acquired popular characteristics and people participated in its many activities. This situation gave me a push and I no longer had any opposition from my parents, especially since my work was praised and I reached a good organizational level.

At the beginning, my commitment to the Revolution was full of enthusiasm, fed by what we heard about the Fedayeen (commandos) and cadres in Jordan and what we read in magazines. Through meetings and events the organization's cause started to take root, and the goals and principles we worked for and which were ongoing were essential elements in the development of my continuing organizational situation.

Our number was very small at the beginning – not more than four or five girls of similar age. After a while we concentrated on students and older women who helped a lot in activities and services for the fighters.

The main occupation of people in the camp was agricultural work, with a small number of petit bourgeois who were UNRWA employees or who followed other careers or worked for contractors. A big percentage of women in the camp worked in the nearby citrus groves. Women's work outside the home contributed to the economic situation of the family and also to social rebellion, even if this was only a small percentage. It made the involvement of women in the Revolution easier. When women are allowed to work outside the home, they are more likely to be allowed to attend meetings or participate in certain camp events. But these activities were not free of obstacles and required great efforts.

BACKGROUND OF THE INHABITANTS OF THE CAMP

The vast majority of the camp inhabitants were from Al-Hola (Al-Ghawarneh). They in particular worked in agriculture. The other part of the camp consisted of groups from many villages in the Galilee and cities in Palestine. People from Hola were looked on as backward compared to those from more sophisticated towns that had better access to communication with the outside world. Moreover, such people used to have their girls work as maids in the homes of rich families in Beirut. So when a girl was eight years old she would have to leave her parents' home. This job was unenviable and considered shameful; it was constantly criticized by the inhabitants of other areas. However, their involvement in the Revolution was large and the percentage of martyrs also was higher than for those from other areas.

There were strong family relations in the camp. People did not need a formal relationship with their neighbours or family members; they could visit each other whenever they liked and exchange whatever they needed. Anyone in need was helped without having to ask, in particular on special occasions or in the season of purveyance.

Some elements helped strengthen social relations between people, among which was the fact that the camp was far from the centre of the capital and the houses were very close to each other.

People had the same needs and were in the same political situation. As for the age of marriage before the Revolution, it was young, 13-15, due to the large number of family members – often from six to thirteen in one family, and so the father would want his daughters to get married, enabling him to be free of the burden and responsibility for them.

In the age of Revolution female education increased, which helped some girls reach high social and educational levels such as that of doctor or teacher. It also contributed to improvements in the economic situation of the family and of girls' marriage conditions. Thus, the marriage age for girls increased to between 18 and 20 years, at the end of preparatory school. Women's involvement in the Revolution became acceptable because of the activities that were achieved.

Social Conditions before and during the Revolution

Having multiple wives was never a social phenomenon either before or after the Revolution; even if it did happen sometimes it was very limited, and was justified [when a marriage had produced no children]. But it did happen a little in the time of the Revolution. It used to happen when a young man who had reached high levels in the Revolution thought that his first wife was no longer suitable for the new phase he had reached and would look for another wife who could keep up with him in his new relationships and new way of life – but this could not be described as a phenomenon.

As for divorce, it was also very limited since it was frowned upon. Even if there was disagreement life would go on in its routine, in particular when there were children who were a responsibility and a bond for the couple, especially the mother. Before the Revolution, marriage would happen in a traditional way: the parents of the couple would choose, and so both husband and wife were done an injustice, especially the wife. Nevertheless, the girl was not violently coerced to marry someone she did not want; but in the absence of love or an alternative, and especially if the girl had a weak personality, the marriage would take place leaving each one to their luck, and except in the cases of very close family ties, such as with cousins, it would happen mostly without the girl being consulted.

During the Revolution and after, the institution of marriage developed alongside the development and advance of awareness, and choosing a spouse became more acceptable, especially since the increase in the marriage age made it possible for the girl to choose with her own best interests in mind. In most cases, but not always, the marriage would take place after the young man and woman had been introduced and there was mutual agreement on future life and issues – although the parents, of course, did not encourage such relations.

As for those who worked in the political domain, relationships would develop in a more modern way whereby the couple would get to know each other closely and matters were discussed scientifically and precisely before there was any bond. But this was not a social phenomenon. There were no high dowries. The dowry sum quoted was acceptable to everyone, except on the very rare occasions where it was indicative of covert refusal. This happened at the onset of the Revolution with the fighters spread out all over the camps and many coming from outside the Galilee area (from the West Bank and Gaza Strip). There were fears that girls would become estranged and marry someone they knew nothing about. Gradually and with time, parents overcame this obstacle and there were many marriages with people from the West Bank and Gaza Strip. This was further encouraged by some of the important notables socially giving their daughters in marriage in this way, and so others began to follow suit.

SENSITIVE PROBLEMS

There were limited cases of prostitutes in the camp. We heard of two girls and three women. The girl and her family were usually boycotted and she would be looked on with disdain. I do not have further information because the camp is small and its relations are clear and for many reasons I could not at the time go deeper into these matters. The parents would be pressured to stop this behaviour by someone close to them. As to how the young men solved their sexual problems, this happened, in my opinion, outside the camp, in the city of Tyre itself and more widely in Beirut where there are more opportunities and people do not know each other, so there was no embarrassment to the young men. I would imagine that is how it was from the absence of the young men and their trips to Beirut at the end of each month, and the covert way they spoke about such matters.

SOCIAL SITUATION AFTER THE FIGHTERS' WITHDRAWAL

Women's situation regressed after the withdrawal of the Revolution from the area in 1982. There was reneging on the reform regarding marriage, and early marriage was practised again for girls and even for boys. This was due to two main reasons:

1. the instability of the security situation as a result of the occupation and the threat of the opposing Lebanese militias (the Phalangist and the Lebanese Forces); also the anxiety and concern for girls due to the Israeli occupation, especially after the events of Sabra and Shatila;
2. the exorbitant increase in the cost of living and the absence of work opportunities, which made the presence of a young woman in the family an economic burden, the solution to which was to give her in marriage where she could also be protected.

90

The positive element of the Revolution was, as I mentioned before, an increase in females' education, a phenomenon that continued. Also work as maids came to an end. This was considered a great achievement and was replaced by agricultural labour and work in various institutions (Secours Populaire, GUPW, Beit Atfal al-Sumoud), which aimed to benefit girls by developing skills such as sewing, stitching and embroidery. This was a personal benefit on the one hand, and a contribution towards increasing the income of the family on the other.

THE EFFECT OF RELIGION IN DAILY SOCIAL AND POLITICAL LIFE

There was no negative influence of religion on the social reality, especially not on women, the proof being that women kept on going out to work and to study, but of course they continued practising religious rituals such as fasting and all that has to do with Islamic values.

Religious currents and organizations benefited from the setback of the Revolution and spread more among people, especially since the Revolution had not realized the ambitions of the masses. In other words, the oppressed reverted to religion hoping to find there the solutions to their problems. This was manifested more obviously in the matter of women's dress, and in encouraging the marriage of religious men to religious women. Despite the spread of this behaviour, it was not practised with coercion and people were not hurt or threatened. The religious men have their ways of persuasion, such as helping the needy, giving presents for the feasts, and distributing money, meat and other temptations to prove their credibility.

THE INFRASTRUCTURE OF THE CAMP BEFORE AND AFTER

The camp lacked social services. For example, sewers were not covered; they were merely open drains. The roads were narrow and not paved. It was difficult to get around, especially by car. The camp lacked medical services, with the exception of the UNRWA clinic. With the onset of the Revolution in the camp there were some social services that helped the Palestinians in more than one way; for example, regarding medication. Three medical centres were established by the Palestinian organizations and the Red Crescent. They offered medicine and first aid and the Crescent's hospital received medical cases at night. There were also several kindergartens which offered educational services to the camp's children. Career opportunities arose for women and the possibility of participation in a social life away from home. A number of qualifying centres were opened to teach sewing, stitching, embroidery and typing, which helped in raising the level of women. Some of these activities started through individual initiatives such as the kindergarten and the sewing centre and, after a while, they were adopted by the GUPW. An artesian well was dug; the sewers were organized and covered; the roads were paved by the popular committees, and there were follow-ups by the cadres until the jobs were completed. Individual shelters were dug inside the houses. The cadres, with their various initiatives, had a major role in achieving many of these things and in joining with people in digging and supplying the necessary materials for free through the popular committees and the organizations. A large number of public shelters were built in the camps.

While the cadres formulated the plans and oversaw their development, ordinary people also made a major contribution. For example, when someone dug a shelter in their house, most of the neighbours would effectively contribute to the extent that it would have been difficult for any passer-by to know who owned it. People would always respond to calls for help in cleaning the rain-sodden and messy shelters and in other tasks such as the sewers and roads. The residents would help the moment we arrived in a certain quarter. Finally, there came a follow-up on the work, evaluation of the achievements in addition to reviews – both good and bad. This was the job of the cadres.

ACTIVITIES IN THE FATAH ORGANIZATION

I progressed in Fatah. I organized periodic visits with the sisters to the fighters at their bases on all national and religious occasions and this had a positive effect on their morale and spirits. We encouraged women in leadership roles and in popular committees, and to contribute to discussions and give their opinion.

As for military work, it was confined to local sessions for the sisters (dismantling and reassembling weapons) during which there were some political lectures. I participated in a two-week training session and in other central sessions outside the camp cadre and in the weekly lectures held centrally by Fatah women's office and the Union in Beirut.

EXPERIENCE IN GUPW

I participated in and supervised many Union activities and first aid sessions – an area it was necessary to concentrate on because of the security situation and the repeated aggressions against the area by the Zionist enemy. We contributed greatly by receiving the wounded and attending to them at the hospital. Our experience in the framework of the GUPW was successful due to several factors: the presence of a good, conscious and understanding cadre; our being far away from the centre (Beirut) and its problems; cooperation with and respect for us on the part of the popular committee and its help in providing us with transport to reach the institutions.

MY EXPERIENCE IN BURJ AL-SHIMALI CAMP DURING THE ISRAELI INVASION ON SUNDAY 6 JUNE 1982

During the Israeli invasion of Lebanon, civilians from Burj al-Shimali, men, women, children, old and young joined with the military to heroically defend their camp. I participated in this confrontation of the invading army. More than 30 military vehicles were destroyed at the entrances to the camp and the Israeli commander of the operation was killed. When the confrontation intensified the enemy escalated the attack with incendiary bombs, destroying more than 70 per cent of the houses. The attacks, targeting mainly on the eastern neighbourhoods, came from land, sea and air, and more than 90 people – mainly women and children – were massacred in the underground shelter of the al-Hola club. Other smaller shelters were also destroyed, resulting in the deaths of dozens of civilians. The leaders defending the camp decided to pull out towards the north and in the ensuing confrontation with the occupying forces a number of fighters fell and others were taken prisoner.

WOMEN'S ROLE AFTER THE ISRAELI INVASION IN 1982

Our work was harder during the Israeli invasion. We moved to secret work. At the beginning we were helping the afflicted and distributing the supplies we got through UNRWA and UNICEF. We also brought allowances to the fighters' families who could not leave the area. Along with some of the most trusted sisters, I contacted some fighters in order to evacuate them safely to the Bekaa area. At the beginning we hid the weapons underground and when an opportunity arose I provided the fighters with what they needed. With my mother and another woman, I provided supplies to some fighters who were still in the area fighting the occupation; we also kept them supplied with the information they needed.

Women's work was concentrated on healing social and psychological wounds and dealing with oppressive enemy practices such as entering houses, corralling young men in the open, and hurting and imprisoning them before their parents' eyes. There were secret meetings to organize, missions to undertake, and the need to keep abreast of news and information. Most families had at least one martyr or wounded member, or a loved one detained in Al-Ansar prison in South Lebanon or, worst of all, missing. We women had to work clandestinely on aid and relief, providing food, clothes and covers for the camp population at a local level, re-opening schools in shelters and semi-built constructions. When people were able to return to their homes, the logistical and psychological support continued, in particular to the parents of martyrs, the wounded and the imprisoned.

Before things settled down in the camp, I found dozens of rifles and some light weapons in the streets and stored them underground in case they might come in useful, as they did on one occasion when a fighter, Bilal, needed some light weapons for operations behind enemy lines. One of these was blowing up a military base in the Buss area with dozens of enemy dead and wounded. Bilal was eventually martyred and we arranged to take the fighters who were with him to the Bekaa where the resistance had its headquarters so that 12 of them were saved.

When things settled down a bit, we reopened the kindergarten and the work centre under the banner of a Lebanese association. We protested against the Israeli enemy by organizing demonstrations, throwing stones, carrying flags, and encouraging children and women to do the same. We also organized sit-ins at the Red Cross, submitted letters demanding freedom for the prisoners and to allow their families to visit them, and called for a cessation of the inhuman practices by the Israelis and for an improvement in the prisoners' situation.

WOMEN AND LEADERSHIP POSITIONS

In general, the contribution of women in the political sphere was good, but they did not have their rights and did not hold leadership positions suited to their capabilities. Each department was represented by one of the sisters, but only to follow up on the women's situation; they were not offered a media job, for example, even if they were qualified for it.

Theoretically, we would always hear of the necessity to address the women's sector, to raise their awareness, mobilize them, and organize their ranks and other such big slogans. But in practice we saw the opposite. There was no honest effort from the leadership to realize these slogans and programmes because this would have given women material capabilities. Most of what women achieved was by their own efforts and those of a few male cadres who were more aware.

On the other hand, the Union tried to contribute to improving women's position, but this was not enough as the Union is an integral part of the PLO and could not manage the organizational fundamentalism and the differences over quotas and distribution of responsibilities. But the Union had some independence — with patience and some concessions it could have achieved more, especially since there were no big political contradictions between the different factions. But it could not pose issues and problems that have to do, for example, with personal status law or other matters — as any decision needs a political party to implement it, and this was not possible in our situation.

This interview was conducted in Damascus in September 1994.

Residents of Burj al-Shimali

6.
AMAL MASRI

Amal Masri's family is from Haifa in Palestine. Born in the fifties, Amal currently lives in Burj al-Brajneh in Lebanon. She had a career as a florist. In her twenties she joined the Democratic Front for the Liberation of Palestine (DFLP), becoming a central committee member until she left the organization in the 1990s. For a time she was vice president of the General Union of Palestinian Women (GUPW) – Lebanon branch. She is known for her military participation in the struggle – the only female among a group of 75 men.

I come from a nationalistic Palestinian family. My mother and brother played a role in Palestine in 1936 [the Palestinian uprising] in Haifa. In 1948 we moved to Sidon and stayed there a while before moving to Beirut. Our lives were like those of all our Palestinian people. My parents would say 'one week - ten days - one month - two months and we will return'. We grew up, studied and reached the age of embarking on life in its different forms – and then the disaster of 1967 happened.

We lived at first in Shiyah and then in Burj al-Brajneh, Ain al-Sikah, near the camp. At school we formed a group of young women and agreed to assume a national role. That was before 1967. In 1967 there were huge demonstrations and we needed a bigger role. We joined the Arab Nationalist Movement along with a group of young Lebanese men. We worked together, distributing pamphlets, writing on walls.

Our centre was the Pioneers Club (al-Riwwad) in Ras el Nabah; we were Lebanese and Palestinians. It was necessary to transport

99

weapons and other things, and so a girl and a boy would take them by car. The first military training session was held in Mukhtara in 1967 in the days of Kamal Jumblat [politician and leader of the Lebanese National Movement], along with the Arab nationalists. I was the only woman among 75 men; I took it in my stride. All the training that took place was with the attitude that we were all brothers and sisters in struggle and there was a common purpose. My parents knew of the training but did not object — perhaps because I was the youngest in our household and the first to enter the national domain; in fact my mother prayed for me.

MILITARY PARTICIPATION

I had had some training on anti-aircraft guns, but I am not one to remain at the base. I am for training to a very high level. In 1976 during the civil war I was on the mortars and B-7s at Beirut's Holiday Inn where we were opposed by young fighters of the Lebanese Forces who were in Ain al-Muraiseh. I held a training session for a group of young women with the aim of relieving the men and protecting our positions when the men were taking a rest. But I do not think women should join military bases in the South of Lebanon.

The experience of Palestinian women was comprehensive, covering mobilization and social aspects. In those early days we had a real problem with the concept of the Palestinian Revolution. It was deemed shameful for girls to join, especially since in our backgrounds it was not only the father who should be listened to, but also the brother, uncle and cousin. This was a major concern in 1967. Shortly after the beginning of the Revolution in Lebanon, the Cairo Agreement [between the Lebanese and the PLO allowing the presence of Palestinian guerrillas in South Lebanon] was signed in 1969. Our role was more than a military one.

At the beginning of the struggle, only 3, 4 or 5 per cent of our girls were able to join the Palestinian Revolution without complications from their families. Marriage and children made it more difficult. At the beginning there were no institutions in the Revolution, i.e. no newspapers, no systems, etc. It was difficult to visit people's houses and you were not very welcome to do so as the Deuxieme Bureau dominated our people, more so those in the camp than those outside. That's why there were problems in the camps. This decreased when Palestinian institutions were established and more young people joined the Revolution. This provided opportunities for work and other things. It was totally different in the mid-1970s.

WOMEN AND SOCIAL TRANSFORMATION

From the beginning of the civil war in Lebanon, in 1975 until 1982, the head of the family and the one who worked was the woman, but we have backward values that are rooted in us. Young people developed, not necessarily at the ideological level, but each in their own domain. Attitudes towards women's status and social concepts developed. I know many men who help with the housework and care for the kids. For many years now, the wife has become a partner whose feelings and wellbeing they care for, especially when she works as well.

It took time for women in general to surmount familial pressures. Their experience was not simple; what helped was that the camps welcomed the Fedayeen and women benefited from this openness and themselves joined. Some of the factions had awareness and a role at the level of mobilization. The importance of women's national role, and their rights, were acknowledged. This varied from one camp to another – all our camps in Lebanon are different: the north is not like the Bekaa, and the Bekaa is not like Beirut. There was a social fabric between the camp and its surroundings and the Lebanese areas that also contributed to this aspect. But I can say that on the family level, women became more developed.

On a personal level, I do not see that either the PLO nor any other organization actually worked for the liberation of Palestinian women in the Palestinian Revolution. The PLO worked to build female cadres to qualify them for leadership of organizational positions; but the liberation of women was not their concern. I am talking at the organizational level, because if the factions had been like that the situation would have been altogether different. We in the same [political] organization used to say there are women at the organizational level whose awareness and qualifications are higher than those the PLO has chosen. There was not a single woman on the executive committee. Why? This is ridiculous. We used to laugh about it.

The major issues in the camps were early marriage and, eventually, early divorce. But this happened in certain periods. During the first war of the camps there was this big wave of marriage/divorce.

After 1982 [the Israeli invasion of Lebanon] there were behavioural issues. There was a serious drug problem in Burj al-Brajneh. Before 1982 this was limited. Prostitution in the full sense of the word was not an issue, but personal moral corruption was.

THE GENERAL UNION OF PALESTINIAN WOMEN

The Women's Union was the framework under which we all gathered. The General Union of Palestinian Women had a problem. The different political organizations represented in the GUPW did not necessarily give priority to the Union's work. One of my problems with the organization of the Democratic Front was the GUPW. The Front did not understand the national framework correctly. The national framework is the umbrella over all our organizations. What does organization mean? To mobilize the capabilities of your people. And though the different factions might differ on how to liberate Palestine, we are all working to this end and we must meet in the middle. If this view is not present, and it is not even until now, the Union remains the national framework for Palestinian women. What do I care for the women's organization of the Democratic or Popular Front? I tell you, Fatah is smarter than us; it considers the GUPW is their women's bureau. In Lebanon it played a major role in solving many problems.

In the period of the Sabra and Shatila Massacres, and after the departure of the PLO from Lebanon, there were huge problems. We were helping families financially and also medically. In these difficult circumstances there were many marriages and divorces in which we would intervene, not just as a Union. The martyrs' families were not sent any money for a while and those with children were the worst cases – yet there was no institution to help them. The amount they were given was doubled to only 100 dollars a month.

I joined the Union in 1973. We did not prioritize the activities of the Union; we did what was possible. We established a restaurant and kindergartens, but there were not many projects because the PLO only supported the restaurant and kindergartens. We did not try to build one productive institution. I had many projects in mind. I even thought of doing this at a personal level, should things get easier for me. A priority would have been a gas station, or a juice shop, a roaster – can anyone do without a cup of coffee, even a bakery? I have always spoken of these projects, why not do them?

In Lebanon the secretariat and the branch had a joint role. Until 1982 the General Secretariat in Lebanon had an important role, even at the political level. We cannot deny its participation in conferences, its political participation, and at the same time the international support it was given. The UN Women's Congress was the first to condemn Zionism and equate it with racism. Unfortunately, this was later rescinded because our leadership policies did not keep up these achievements.

103

Role during Siege of Beirut in 1982

There was the grassroots struggle of the people in the camps and outside, supported by the Union. I had a rich experience with others during the Israeli siege of Beirut in 1982. Fadia represented the Union in Burj al-Brajneh and the Haret Hreik area and formed several groups, then we divided up the area. We had a military group of guards, and food was provided for all. We formed a social committee and a health committee. There was a special committee to visit air raid shelters, to check on sick people and provide them with the medicines they needed. Most important of all was that the whole area was covered. Being able to get hold of bread was a big thing. We used to fill little trucks with bread and other supplies and the driver would distribute it to the whole area. The Union played a major role in this. Even now when I meet people, they tell me, 'you remember, Amal, you sent us supplies in '82'. A while ago I was in a service taxi and the driver asked me, 'Aren't you Amal?' On one occasion we opened up a flour warehouse, took all the flour to the bakeries, and then distributed the bread. All this was paid for and it's important that some people still remember. When there is a harmonious group with one goal the work is very successful.

I remember Martin and a group of foreigners got us the six-wheel truck to Haret Hreik. Once, they even brought the truck when the airplanes had been shelling for 14 hours. Those are the foreigners who helped us – they came the day of a 14-hour bombardment!

I told the group to sit in a safe place while we emptied the six-wheeler. They looked at us wondering if we were mad, but we knew the area. What I mean is that, when there is a clear and specified goal and there are no problems, everyone has a role. At that time Shadia was in charge of the branch, and all the roles were distributed. It was a very successful experience for the Union, which did not encroach on anyone's authority. We had military patrols – not a small number; I cannot remember now, but the minimum was about 75 women.

ROLE AFTER PLO WITHDRAWAL

We kept up the same momentum after the PLO's withdrawal in 1982, and after the massacre of Sabra and Shatila. The situation in Sabra and Shatila following the massacre was terrible; the camp was invaded by dogs and cats. People returned to the camp because they had a bond with it. They had been born and raised in the camp, they had lived and given birth there; and many in their families had died there. Some families had been there for 30 years, and they had long memories.

WAR OF THE CAMPS

In the war of the camps the Women's Union played an important role. Amneh and I are still living. It started on May 20, 1985, the first day of Ramadan. I went into the camp – people wondered how we had managed to do so under sniper fire. We took stock of all the shops and made a warehouse for the Union. All the Union members gathered together.

I stayed a month and a week during the first battle. Right at the beginning, Amal [a Lebanese political party behind the attacks on the camps] came to the house and took my car. At all stages we would work as the GUPW, providing food for the young men, helping the wounded, and recruiting women to assist the Red Crescent. No one had a problem when we stayed in their homes. The relationship was clear, and many of the Palestinian organizations participated.

PLO and Social Change

I think we could have changed laws, especially the personal status laws such as polygamy and the custody of children, had there been a coordinated working group who really believed in the struggle to achieve some of our rights – even if this was outside the Union's General Assembly or Administrative Committee. On the political level our representation within the framework of the PLO was insufficient. On the social level we should have worked harder to leave something for the next generation.

The interview was conducted in Beirut in September 2007.

Al Sanayeh building, Beirut,
destroyed by Israeli vacuum bomb, 1982

7.

MAJIDA MASRI

Majida is a qualified chemistry teacher who worked in Jordan where she became a member of the Democratic Front for the Liberation of Palestine (later a member of its political bureau). She had been exiled to Jordan from Nablus in Palestine. She then went to Lebanon to join the struggle there. She was on the Administrative Committee of the General Union of Palestinian Women and, from 2015 to the present day, on its General Secretariat. Following her time in Lebanon, she eventually returned to Nablus and became Minister of Social Affairs in the Palestine Authority Government from 2009 till 2013. Her writings include articles and working papers on women's and political issues. She reflects on the difficulties in bringing together the goals of the umbrella organization, the GUPW, and those of the women's groups in other factions. The question of prioritizing between social and national aims is a perennial one that constantly arose in the daily struggle. Majida sees that inequality between men and women is still possible in a leftist organization.

I can say that the Palestinian disaster, the displacement and the cause were my whole life. My family is from Nablus, but my father's work and the family's life were in Haifa, so we left like all Palestinian refugees when I was in the first months of my life.

The town of Haifa was present in our house every day: my grandmother, father and sister would talk about it. My sister would always draw our house in Haifa, and my father spoke about his work there with pride. He was an important businessman – but after the displacement he was penniless, and it got worse when my mother died in 1951 and he had to bear the responsibility of five children.

Daily I opened my eyes suffering the loss of my mother, and the feeling of deprivation grew when I also felt the loss of my home country. I knew that my mother would not come back, but I was sure that the home country would. Early on, when I was a student in first secondary, I joined the Arab Nationalist Movement [ANM] where there were people older than me. I respected them. They became my role models: my older brother, my neighbours and teachers at the school.

We were influenced at the time by nationalism and Nasserism that were spreading widely, and betting on Arab unity to liberate Palestine and facilitate our return to Haifa, Jaffa and Acre. The defeat of 1967 shocked us all. We discovered that it was a losing bet and were convinced that only we ourselves could do it. The choice before us was to join the resistance movement. In September 1968 the occupying forces came to the house to arrest me a day after I had left Nablus, so I couldn't return.

The atmosphere of the family was comforting – it was patriotic and democratic. My mother died when I was four, so my father, grandmother and sister raised us; my sister married when I was in sixth elementary, so I and my three brothers managed our affairs, cooperating in everything. There was no division of labour between a boy and a girl – my brothers grew up this way, and remained so with their wives and children.

My father did not differentiate between boys and girls – which was very important in my life – maybe because he was directly responsible for us, replacing our mother. We did not have the traditional conflict of authority between father and mother in the house. More than that, my father had a clear position: he would say that, since I was cleverer than my brothers, I had priority for higher education. Education for my father, as for all Palestinian refugees, was the most important, the most significant thing in his life. He wanted us all to be taught at university – with the exception of my eldest sister, who had married after leaving secondary school, although his financial situation was poorer than average, and the circumstances of our education were very difficult.

My father knew about me and my brothers' nationalist activities, and like any father he was always worried about us, but he never interfered to prevent us from participating in those activities. He would sometimes express his worry with questions, remarks and cautioning.

From the beginning national activity was the clear choice for me, without any hesitation. Maybe when a woman hesitates she gives her husband or brother the chance to interfere, but if she has made a decision and a clear commitment, she doesn't hesitate. Nothing will hinder her struggle, neither engagement, nor giving birth, nor work, nothing affects her. I am talking about those classified as cadres. From our experience of the women with whom we worked, we know how hard and complicated it is for them, who suffer and are weak at certain periods in their lives.

I went to Jordan in 1970 after graduating from university. I came with my family to Lebanon in 1976 at the call for the general mobilization of the PLO and the Democratic Front during the siege of Tal al-Zaatar camp. We travelled in a small boat with a number of incomers to Lebanon by sea from the port of Limassol in Cyprus to Sidon. It was of course a big risk, because we could have been attacked by the Israeli boats or the Phalangist at any moment. It was a journey of terror, one of the hardest moments of my life. I lived constantly a conflict between my national duty and my responsibility for my children, and I would always make a balance or go for the priority of the moment's need. That time at sea, I honestly did not recognize the nature of the danger. I confess to that now.

THE PALESTINIAN CAUSE AND WOMEN'S CAUSE
ARE INTERCONNECTED

My concentrated women's experience began in Lebanon, because the party's aim was to build a women's organization. Our organization was divided into groups (women-youngsters-workers). I did not find a role for myself outside the framework of women's work and its party committees, in what this means for a popular, national and political role connected to daily missions. For me this is crucial because the national work with women is a necessary condition for developing their role in the national movement, apart from its being the course of action of the organization. Briefly I consider I have two causes: the national cause, which is the main cause, and the women's cause within it, and the two are interconnected.

The beginning of my experience in the General Union of Palestinian Women (GUPW) was when I became a member of the Administrative Committee for Lebanon branch in 1977 as a representative of the Democratic Front (DFLP), and I remained in this position until 1982 when I left Lebanon. In the GUPW congress of 1980 in Beirut I became a member of its administrative council, a position I still hold at the time of writing.

PROUD OF MY EXPERIENCE IN THE GUPW IN LEBANON

My experience in the Union in Lebanon was very important and I am proud of it. I was in the position where I wanted to be, which went well with my interests: work within a national unified women's framework. This was enriched by grassroots experience, and I think I contributed positively, in complete harmony with myself and with the policy of my organization. Of course, this was alongside my colleagues in the Union from other factions [organizations affiliated to PLO]. My companions in the

Democratic Front sometimes said that I represented the GUPW in the Front rather than the opposite!

My convictions were strengthened through our experience in Lebanon branch: that common daily work shortens the distance between the women of the factions, and contributes to building healthy national relations based on respect, creating space for dialogue, accepting differences and listening to other opinions. This was in spite of huge difficulties, and sometimes suffering, because of the formula of $1 + \frac{1}{2}$ for Fatah, as a norm or law, which made voting the formula for solving differences. The membership of the Union at the time was close to 25,000. The Union built an organizational body with committees in all the places where there were Palestinian camps and residence. This enabled the expansion of the number of the local, middle and leadership cadres working in the Union. This is very important, but it was not repeated in the experience of the Union in other branches, remembering that at the time the Lebanon branch was the largest.

We made sure that the programme we posed in the DF women's organization was the same that we posed in the Union, so there would be no contradiction. But those activities that we could not pass through the Union we carried out with our own resources be they political or social. I remember, for example, with regard to the celebrations of 8 March – International Women's Day – some officials wanted to have their own [organizational] celebrations. We in the Women's Union wanted to raise the slogan that March 8 would be a national Palestinian day. All March 8 celebrations took place through the GUPW, and we had a separate internal celebration for our own organization (the DF), but the popular celebrations had to be through the women's national framework.

THERE WAS NO BIG CONFLICT OVER DEMOCRATIC VALUES
IN THE INSTITUTIONS OF THE PLO

In the evaluation sessions we would say this, but it was not practically translated. In the PLO National Council or popular conferences of the unions we would say that the conflict was over the political aspects; all efforts with regard to a paragraph here or there, or over the leadership formations and the shares [quotas] of the organizations, was a necessary conflict because our battle was political. But the democratic aspect that has to do with the institutions of the PLO and its structure, the future of its work, and specifically to do with the mechanism of decision-making, were all led by the decisions of Fatah – not only by its rejection of quotas but also by its views on the essence of the concept of democracy. We established the formula of half +1(majority) for Fatah and the rest for everybody else. We boast of democracy in Palestinian society and the PLO but in the end we did not create any serious democratic situations in the institutions of the PLO in any true sense. We are reaping the results in politics and in the decision-making committees.

GUPW EXPERIENCE IN EMERGENCY

The experience of the war from two standpoints – the aggression (1978 invasion of southern Lebanon) and the 1982 aggression – was important in establishing joint national work, specifically with the displaced. Special committees were formed which worked in various missions starting with visits to assess needs and to provide assistance and offer services. Also in 1982 GUPW members played an important role in offering the necessary provisions which the Red Crescent and UNRWA supplied to residential areas, distributing them via members in the different locations, specifically Burj al-Brajneh and the suburbs which were heavily bombarded in an attempt to isolate those areas from Beirut. This was in addition to the missions of Union members in their different areas.

THE RELATIONSHIP: THE NATIONAL AND THE SOCIAL

On the subject of the social and the national, and one winning over the other, in that period the national was ahead of the social in daily activities. The mobilization of women, however, happened mainly through social projects, in the sense that women participated in programmes that could lead to a career, like sewing, or in the membership of a cultural or health committee, or through councils of mothers in kindergartens. But we were living in a sensitive political period. The PLO defended itself and its existence and its sole representation of its people and national rights, in the face of Israeli invasions and attempts to destroy its identity, with the existence of martyrs, wounded and families of militias and fighters. And so the national mission took priority without question.

The grassroots centres of the union worked with various social activities, but without a clear vision of the nature of the social missions connected to the rights and causes of women – as females – outside the framework of the rights and duties of Palestinian women to participate in the national role. Even the social committees that were formed worked mainly on social projects related to national concerns, such as caring for the families of martyrs, fighters, the displaced and wounded.

We considered giving attention to women by building a women's union that would mobilize and organize them within a national programme. The number of women who might reach the national council and positions of political leadership was taken for granted as a crowning of the presence of women's participation in the popular base and in the organization. This matter was not one of dispute for the factions in the sense of the numbers of women in these positions, because what is important is the presence of those who represent the thought and position of the organization itself in these committees. There was no enlightenment and awareness platform for the comrades with regard to the women's cause and the absence at the time of enlightened feminist thought. The factions did not make the battle for democracy within the institutions of the PLO, which is the largest platform for the issue of women's democratic rights.

The DFLP wouldn't intervene in issues such as marriage, divorce, multiple wives and caring for children, unless the person concerned asked for it, and these are limited cases. If there was something big, then there would be intervention. Multiple wives was a personal matter and the cases were very limited.

It is not true that the DF preferred marriage to be between two people from the same organization, although maybe some individual comrades did, and this is healthy for daily and married life. In some cases a woman would be accepted as a comrade but, when married, she became simply a housewife, and no longer a comrade.

When the DFLP split [into two factions], only one couple, who are known because they are leaders, had their differences and divorced, even though they remained on good terms. The rest of the wives followed their husbands, or either did or didn't reach an understanding with them.

It is important to mention that the women comrades were represented in all organizational committees of the Front. A number of comrades achieved the first official positions through their qualifications.

Of course there are some comrades who are backward socially – with apologies to the comrades – and this shows through their behaviour towards the wife, sister or female comrades, which makes us wonder sometimes: is this possible in a leftist organization? This happens, and we understand it from the position that changing social values and behaviour needs a long time, and it does not happen just by being in a leftist organization. The paradox is when a comrade is in an official position and holds female comrades accountable for their performance and role, and at the same time forbids his wife or sister from effective participation.

MY FAMILY

As for my family, my marriage failed. I had married someone from the same organization. There was no contradiction with my national choice, and there was no problem with my being in the organization. But whether we like it or not the contradiction between man and woman in our society reflects itself somehow in the family. Without entering into personal details, in general what the husband read or learned in the organization about the rights of women and her position in society is not enough. It may be important, but in the end upbringing and the customs and values of society influence his behavior, which could be cruel and manifest backwardness. It could create a conflict for him between the values and culture he gained and the upbringing he had, because mostly in our society the man deals with the natural rights of women as though they are privileges. But I don't think that the failure of my married life had anything to do with my involvement in the organization and my political work. I say this to my children, not to justify it, because even if we had been outside the struggle our married life would have failed. We couldn't continue with each other because of our different personalities. It just did not work for us. We met when we were working in the national struggle and the organization, and we separated also like this … and we are still working in the organization.

The interview was conducted in Amman in September 1994.
Majida rewrote it (with some additions and deletions) in May 2008.

8.
WADAD QOMRI

One of the women pioneers, from initially clandestine political activity as a teenager in Jerusalem, Wadad's commitment to the Palestinian cause remained a constant throughout her life. And like many before her, her journey took her through Jordan to Damascus and hence to Lebanon. At the time of the interview she was living in Amman. Beyond her work as a teacher and as a librarian at the PLO Research Centre, she was a member of Popular Front for the Liberation of Palestine and instrumental in helping to set up students' and workers' unions and, not least, the GUPW, where she was a member of the administrative committee in the Lebanese branch. Her long desired project to see the establishment of family law, which would have been to the benefit of women, met many obstacles such as the Lebanese Civil War and ceded place to more urgent matters. Despite many women pioneers, says Wadad, women's contribution to the Revolution was not given the acknowledgement it merited, and their representation in leadership roles was almost non-existent.

My interest in politics began when I was a student at school in Jerusalem in the 1950s. Jordan witnessed much political momentum (1956-1958) at that time. Many projects were suggested: the project of Palestinian housing at Al Aghwar, diversion of waters of the Jordan River, and others in the period of Al Nabulsi's government – which did not last long but saw many movements. I was in secondary school when I began to participate in demonstrations, and that led to my organized activities within the framework of the Arab National Movement.

119

My family is a middle class family; they were open-minded socially, which meant that they didn't place restrictions on movement in general, even though the participation of girls in a political movement in that period was unacceptable on all levels, it being a matter for men only. I myself didn't face such a problem, but I was carrying a big burden. I had to gradually gain my parents' trust and accept their guidance, which called for caution and abiding by the habits and traditions of the surrounding environment. As this was a secret activity, so was the movement secret and limited. For example, I began my activities in Jerusalem. The number of female party members was very limited, so we women all knew one another, the prevailing parties being the Communist Party, the Baath Party and the Arab National Movement. In women's ranks specifically, their expansion was limited. I was the first official in Amman. Female members of the movement were mainly students coming in summer from outside Jordan. They reinforced our work during that period, and activities increased. Thereafter we concentrated on secondary school students and teachers, including teachers returning from abroad who played the biggest role, as they had a strong influence due to their many connections.

We started to think of broadening the scope of our work. Following the establishment of the PLO, our aim was to establish the General Union of Palestinian Women (GUPW). It held its first congress in Jerusalem. We also founded and joined other unions: the students' union and the workers' union. I, for example, was enrolled in the University of Damascus, so I joined the students' union, and later the teachers' union. I worked mainly in the women's union. We started work in the villages, taking into consideration that villagers had their own habits and traditions.

I was on the Jerusalem committee and participated in the general congress. I was one of the founders of the Union's (GUPW) branch in Jordan. After the PLO centres and its institutions were closed by a decision of the Jordanian regime, we went back to secret activities.

PARTICIPATION IN THE STRUGGLE AFTER THE 1967 OCCUPATION

After the 1967 war the national movement began to re-establish its connections and we started with high morale and strong enthusiasm. Activities in the Revolution were a continuation of the national movement, proof of that being when people would come from the suburbs and villages saying 'You taught us what to do'. And so it could be said that in 1967 we didn't start from scratch but continued what we had been doing before. Although the administration was not widespread, it was effective, and women began to assume a pioneering role. The first statement calling for a boycott of Israeli products was issued by women and they had a major role in keeping people from leaving the country. Then it was necessary to re-establish the organizational bodies and to participate in the Revolution in different forms. The Israeli enemy initially did not pay much attention to women's struggle, but after a few operations they began to make arrests.

Following our involvement in this military activity we went to Jordan for training, and here it was harder to keep people inside the Occupied Territory after the military training. So the target became across the river and this was one of our main missions to build the organizational operation. This was more important than military activity for us because it ensured the continuation of the struggle.

Sometimes objective circumstances obliged some of us to leave the occupied land, and that happened to me. I left Jerusalem in 1968 and stayed in Amman for a while to watch the situation inside, and then I left, taking the advice to cut the thread which the enemy might be holding and benefiting from.

In Jordan I worked in the women's sector. The decision at the time was to work through the organization itself and not through the unions. The participation of women in the struggle at higher levels became more acceptable socially and so they began arms training, going to military camps and sleeping outside the home. The Revolution provided women with the possibility of a certain degree of progress. The participation of women became normal, even in some operations.

I moved to Lebanon and followed up on women's work in 1971-1972. The atmosphere was ready for the re-establishment of the GUPW in Lebanon, where a bourgeois mentality was exemplified in a leadership similar to that of philanthropic associations and did not accord with our work and its requirement: the reality of armed struggle. Then came the struggle to revolutionize the Union after the proof of the failure of this bourgeois outlook and its practices, mostly after the Lebanese Army's attack on the camps. The role of the Union was greater than that and was connected to the Palestinian Revolution in all its dimensions – political, economic and social. This is what happened during the congress and the formation of a new administrative committee in 1973. Attention was given to the political aspect and the branches started assuming their role too.

WOMEN'S LIBERATION AND LEADERSHIP POSITIONS

Even though all the organizations posed this matter at different levels, and despite the presence of women pioneers who were assuming their roles, representation in the leadership did not equate to women's level of participation in the struggle. The Union did not assume a role in social issues that reflected women's issues outside the political realm. The Palestinian Revolution was not settled in one place and did not allow for strong foundations that might enhance women's situation. It was based in several different countries. The many wars and the movement of its cadres from one place to another prevented the Revolution from laying down such foundations. The divisions within the Palestinian Revolution did not serve the Union.

In 1975-1976 we made a long study of a project for family law that would improve the lot of Palestinian women to be submitted to the PLO, which had the authority to impose such a law on the fighters and members of all organizations. But events intervened – mainly the civil war in Lebanon and the priorities imposed by social issues, issues of the wounded and families of martyrs as well as the basic demands of defending the Revolution.

From the beginning the Popular Front had a clear and positive position on women which led to them reaching leadership positions. For example, International Women's Day and its reflection was a long and continuing struggle, but this achievement was not reflected on each member of the Front.

The Palestinian Revolution elevated the status of Palestinian women at all levels – social, economic and educational. I can conclude that our role was elevated but remained less than what we had aspired to.

The interview was conducted in Amman in October 1994.

9.

Hasna Rida

Originally from Bint-Jbeil in Southern Lebanon near the border with Palestine, Hasna now lives in Beirut. She joined Fatah in 1968 as a student at Beirut College for Women, becoming a member of the students' committee. She was assistant researcher at the Planning Centre Education Department from 1972 to 1976. Her interview highlights the changes in attitude that have taken place towards women in a movement which put national liberation first. She became director of the children's publisher Dar al-Fatah al-Arabi, based in Cairo, until 1993 and was a founding member and executive manager of Nour – Arab Women's Publishing in Egypt from 1993 to 2008, producing a quarterly newsletter. She now works with several NGOs that address different Palestinian issues.

My Path to the Resistance

Palestine had been in our lives since I was born. I am from Bint Jbeil and was born in 1947. My maternal grandfather had friends and partners in his work in Palestine. His partner's whole family came to live with us before 1948. The family consisted of father, mother, seven children, the father's sister and the mother's sister. They all lived in the diwan (hall) of my grandfather's house in Bint Jbeil. We grew up with them around us until 1956. One of my maternal uncles was an officer in the army and another was a police officer; my eldest maternal uncle was a doctor who graduated in the 1940s and was among the first from Bint Jbeil to join the Baath Party when he was at the American University. He and Nimr

125

Toukan were in the Aid Unit of the Rescue Army [Arab Liberation Army]. When the Rescue Army came to Malikiyya, the gathering was in Bint Jbeil in front of my grandfather's house under the leadership of Fawzi al-Kawakji [Commander of the Rescue Army]. Of course we were young then. We knew that the eldest son of the Palestinian Ayyoubi family, Fakhri al-Ayyoubi, was a commando. He would execute an operation against Israel and return to sleep at the house and then we didn't see him. Although we were very young, this commando remained in our imagination as someone mysterious.

In 1956, the Israelis planted a bomb in the house to kill him. It exploded at dawn that day. My maternal uncles, who were officers, were visiting us for the weekend and I remember exactly that at 4 or 5 o'clock in the morning the inhabitants of Bint Jbeil, many in their pyjamas, came to our house. We didn't understand what had happened, whether anyone had died or not; but we knew, thank God, that Fakhri was OK as the window fell over his face and protected him. The next day the whole family decided to leave and move to Ain al-Hilweh [Palestinian refugee camp near the city of Sidon] so as not to expose us to more danger.

My father had emigrated to Nigeria in 1952 and my mother remained to keep the house open. That year she decided we should go to boarding school so that she could follow my father. This was five years after his emigration. We went to Souk el Gharb – my maternal uncle was an officer in the nearby city of Aley. The school was famous, especially as it attracted students from all the Arab countries, Iraq, Saudi Arabia and Jordan. Of course, there were many Palestinians, Kuwaitis, and Lebanese whose parents were emigrants or from the inhabitants of the village of Souk al-Gharb itself. The school's president was Tawfiq Khabbaz, God rest his soul, whose father, a famous religious man, was Reverend Hanna Khabbaz from Homs. Tawfiq became the director of the school while his assistant was Ahmad Shafiq al-Khatib from Gaza, later head of the Dictionaries and Translation Division at the *Librarie du Liban*.

I went to this school at the age of nine and once a week we had an assembly to talk about a certain subject. I remember Ahmad al-Khatib's first speech in November of that year was about the Balfour Declaration. I would always, with my Palestinian sentiments, look for the Palestinians at school. I felt close to them. Al-Khatib was an Arab nationalist and inspired us all. We always organized demonstrations in Souk al-Gharb for the liberation of Algeria and against the Balfour Declaration. The school was open and liberal and there was effective Arab national activity. In 1965, the year of my graduation, we organized the first book exhibition and invited Dr. Fayez Sayegh [Palestinian-American academic, founder of Palestine Research Centre in Beirut] to give a lecture, as well as Dr. Walid Khalidi [Palestinian historian and co-founder of the Institute for Palestine Studies in Beirut and Washington]. We formed a branch of the Palestinian Students Union.

After graduating I went to Beirut University College for Women (BUC), where there was no political activity. There were girls only and most of them came from the bourgeoisie, or were daughters of ambassadors or ministers from the Arab countries, and their concerns were far from mine; maybe in the boarding school there was interaction with political issues and its concerns, but at BUC, the restrictions constrained them more and their concerns were not political.

The situation changed after the 1967 war. The academic year ended and we weren't to have our final exams until later. Faisal al-Husseini [a prominent Palestinian leader who died in 2001] came with Major Mohammad al-Sha'er and opened the first training camp in a villa in Kayfoun. The event attracted 400 male and female students. Tamam al-Akhal [Palestinian artist and educator] was with us, and also Bassam Abu Sharif [former PFLP member, later adviser to Arafat]. There were students from all the universities, including Lebanese, and Arabs from various countries.

The war broke out in June and we joined the camp in July for 6 weeks.

We discovered there were organizations we did not know about: Fatah and the Popular Front came to attract students who were with Faisal. The students were considered fertile yeast for politicization. I was recruited by Fatah and although BUC was a college for women, we were more directed, maybe the first cell of Fatah, towards joint national activity than to the cause of women. We didn't want a women's union and we insisted on not distinguishing between female and male students: we got what we wanted. However, from the beginning Salwa Mikdadi and I wanted to work in the camp. We worked in Shatila and in Tal al-Zaatar. Our participation with women on social and political issues was important. When we were at the college, there was effective participation in demonstrations against Israel and a leading committee of all students. A famous strike continued for two weeks against the Israeli aggression against Beirut airport when they destroyed the planes [1969]. Yes, a two-week strike!

Tawfiq Khabbaz came to the BUC to ask me to call off the strike, but I convinced him not to. I told him that when students have specific demands the strike shouldn't be ended without anything being achieved, and there was no benefit in ending the strike now. He said to have seminars instead. I told him we were ready to do so. We held seminars about Israel and its dangers in south Lebanon. We invited Major Sweid and he talked about the Litani river and Israel's greed for its waters. We invited Asma Toubi (Palestinian writer) and George Ghanem (Lebanese poet). This happened at the end of a whole week dedicated to Palestine at the university. We held a book exhibition for the Palestinian Research Centre, a week of activities with Fairuz [popular Lebanese singer], songs for Palestine, plays for Palestine, and a mjaddara (lentil) supper in the university garden, and donations for the resistance. There was an exhibition of paintings by Palestinian,

Lebanese and Arab artists living in Lebanon, in which Waddah Fares, Aaref al-Rayyis and Rafiq Sharaf participated — paintings all about Jerusalem or expressing the resistance. At the time there was strong support by artists and authors for the resistance as the Battle of Karameh [when the joint forces of the Jordanians and Palestinians engaged the Israeli Army] had taken place in 1968 and this provided the artists with compelling subjects about the resistance against Israel and the possibility of beating Israel. Umm Jihad [Fatah woman leader] visited us at the exhibition. This created a nationalistic political atmosphere in the university not witnessed until then. There was more interaction and some excellent donations.

DYNAMIC CHANGE

Looking back now, this change in the role of the university student was very positive, and although I had been involved in the Palestinian cause since I was born, actually joining the resistance movement as a member gave me a big push. The students and teachers supported my role. I ran for any committee in the students' union, and I would always be elected president of the social services committee. We fearlessly called for strikes. The students' committee even met with the Lebanese Interior Minister, Sheikh Pierre Gemayel [of the right wing Phalangist party], demanding protection and arming of the South of the country. He told us: 'you are demanding a strong army to protect the South etc…but our strength is in the United Nations; we are weak and our weakness is our strength. So please do not mess it up.' We left the ministry in anger – this encounter made us aware of much that was going on politically in the country.

The role of the university in society made us always initiate and be open to any political changes taking place. We were not separate from society. We used to have work camps in villages in the South or in faraway places. There were also seminars to raise awareness about the Zionist danger to Lebanon and the importance of supporting the Palestinian resistance as a patriotic and national role.

I felt this change and it changed the lives of many girls. I remember on weekends, mainly Saturday nights, most girls who were allowed by their parents to go out wanted to go to the cinema or to a night club; they wanted to dance etc... After 1967, we said that those who joined the organization should not – everything had to be serious work for the cause. Of course this was not necessary, but with our enthusiasm we felt that all our time off from the university should be given to the resistance and not be wasted on secondary matters.

I saw the national cause had priority over the cause of women, and that women's liberation would be accomplished with national liberation. This was not questionable, as long as there was continuity, for sure there would be changes. There was, of course, the empowerment of women, and I felt this support when I joined the resistance, because there was respect on the part of the Palestinian cadres and leaders for the role of women.

We started with educational and cultural activities. We gave lectures to raise awareness, on the history of Palestine, the danger of Zionism, etc. All the camp residents saw this as positive and had no worries about their daughters joining the movement. This was at the beginning. I am talking about 1969, before Abu Ammar came to Lebanon, i.e. before September of Amman [when there were clashes between the Jordanian army and Fedayeen]. These beginnings were cautious and positive. Then came the 'Revival of the Camp – al Inaash' [an educational and heritage NGO] and other organizations. There were clinics and health care and people had more trust and thus allowed their daughters to be involved. This took place in late 1969-70. By 1970, the camp was no longer controlled by the Lebanese Army and the Deuxieme Bureau [Lebanese intelligence] but by the Palestine Armed Struggle Command.

I started working at the Planning Centre. There was a problem in Tal al-Zaatar: there were no sewers, no bathrooms. This was the Planning Centre's main project – a basic service for camp inhabitants. Donations came from wealthy Palestinians in Lebanon.

SOCIAL CONDITIONS IN THE CAMP

What was surprising at first was the conservatism. The economic situation was shocking to the extent that you would be embarrassed about what to wear when visiting them. I used to feel that I shouldn't wear a different thing every time. If you wanted to be accepted, you had to wear either trousers or a long skirt; you know in the 1970s there were mini skirts. My whole life style changed when I went to work in the camp. I no longer thought about my appearance. I was criticized for wearing jeans and having a pack of cigarettes in my pocket. I no longer went to expensive restaurants but to cheap restaurants and donated the difference to something important for the camp. Or we might buy books for them. My whole behaviour changed; not just my outer appearance, but also my economic and social activities. The camp was very sensitive towards appearances and people's behaviour – you know how people instinctively understand the essence of the situation.

Many things were done at the Planning Centre. They even raised awareness in the camp. One of the benefits of being in the Planning Centre was that I was introduced to Mohammad (my husband). Mohammad used to teach at the Lebanese University and volunteered with the Scientific Department at the Planning Centre. He used to come to the Centre in the evenings. He worked with Hassan, Afif and Elias, part of a large group who returned from America after 1967. They formed a studies section dealing with evaluation, appraisals and scientific research, within the concept of operational research and so on.

From 1968 to 1970, most of the movement's finances came from

131

donations which students gathered from universities, and an organization was also formed in secondary schools. After 1970, the situation changed and we no longer relied on the [general population] for funding. This was basic, because it made people participate. There was an organic connection. Imagine if this was still going on – we wouldn't now be begging from America and Europe, and Oslo would not have happened [controversial Accords with Israel which left out the crucial matters of the status of Jerusalem, Israeli settlements in occupied Palestinian territory and Palestinian refugees.]

THE CAUSE OF WOMEN

Maybe because we girls were older, and my father emigrated when I was only five years old, we did not feel that priority was given to the boys, either in responsibility towards us or in education. On the contrary, my father travelled, and the four of us were in the same school where there was co-education. My father did not ask us girls to follow him to Nigeria. My sister married early. When I asked to continue my education, there was a problem in that I was now 18 years old. My parents were in Nigeria and I was being asked for in marriage. I was here in Lebanon without my parents, who felt they had a problem with the relatives here. So they asked me to join them in Nigeria, which I did – but I insisted on continuing my education. I stayed for six months and refused to marry. This insistence made my father send me back. I asked my maternal uncle, who was a doctor, to intercede so that I could continue my studies after the sophomore class. In the end, my father even told me to go and study for my PhD, and he attended the graduation ceremony. This change happened gradually – there were barriers at first, but they all disappeared.

Towards Women's Liberation

In the Planning Centre we were a mixed group and because planning was distributed according to specialization, those who stood out were the ones who succeeded in their particular field, women or men. There was no discrimination at all against women with regard to promotion or moving to a higher level.

However, with every election for the Fatah movement's conference we would discuss why there were fewer women, although there were female cadres who were involved, smart, giving and as ready as men to take office. You would notice that the higher you went in the political leadership, the fewer women who were present. There was encouragement and acceptance of women in speeches, but there was nothing of this on the ground, neither in politics nor in the elections or anything: not in conference, not in the executive committee, and not in the central committee. All women who became members got there because their husbands were martyrs, not because they were elected or because the leadership acknowledged their role. In the official system you can say that women did not have much of a role and in most of the unions their representation was very limited, including in the Students' Union. I remember Mohammad Dajani remained the Student Union's representative for eight years; he would move from one specialization to another to remain in the position of authority. I don't know if the leadership asked him to or if he decided this himself.

As for educated men, most of them, with very few exceptions, admired the struggle of the women as long as she was not their wife. She is great, good and has accomplished things etc., but when she becomes the wife there would be complaints about negligence around the house and marital duties, with the children and socially. The man would be the activist, give lectures, take on an extra job with many duties and conferences to attend, but you, woman, as a cadre, are not equal because you are required to do other things (house and children).

This changed with time, even in regard to household duties. I tell you that the changes I saw in my life between 1968 and the 1980s were leaps forward – the wife was able to convince her husband of the women's cause and that her work was of equal value to his, that housework was equal in value to the struggle outside the home. Why should she bear all these burdens and her husband not contribute? She would not accept to be looked down upon. Either she convinced him through her awareness, practices and respect, and made him respect her role, or the general circumstances changed and it became shameful for him to say he would not participate in housework. There was a change. Now it is normal for a married man to participate in housework, in raising the children and baby-sitting. It is not just the mother's role; he, too, can baby-sit and teach [his children]. I see the change that happened in society, and if this was not the original plan of the Palestinian Revolution, it was certainly the result of this long process which changed the roles of both.

I was among the lucky few. Mohammad was encouraging and accepting. Of course, the problems got bigger when we had children. I used to work forty hours a week and he eleven hours at the university. So he bore the responsibility of raising the children until kindergarten age because he had more free time than I did. We used to participate in committees, activities and evaluations. Mohammad's friends respected my role and they would joke about the fact that I did not cook.

However, if there had been awareness at leadership level that women's liberation was a priority and a basic right, there would have been more positive outcomes and achievements. One of the problems was that the main roles in the Revolution were not given to the intellectual members.

The interview was concluded in Beirut, September 2007.

Samed factory established by PLO

10.
SAMIRA SALAH

At the time of the interview Samira Salah was living in Beirut with her husband and four children. She was originally from a patriotic family in Tiberias, Palestine, who were forced out in 1948 like so many Palestinians. The road from Tiberias led first to Irbid in Jordan, where the family settled, and later they moved to Syria where Samira met her husband-to-be and, in 1970, the two of them moved to Ain al-Hilweh camp in Lebanon where Samira continued along the political path she had begun as a teenager some years before. She describes the 1970s as the golden age of women's work when she was active on several committees. Her employment was with the Palestinian Research Centre. Apart from being on the General Secretariat of the GUPW, she was director of the Department of Refugees' Affairs, a member of the Popular Front for the Liberation of Palestine Central Committee, and of the Administrative Committee of the Pan Arab Women's Union. At the time of the interview, she was a member of the Administrative Committee, Social Interaction Centre and the Right of Return Organization. However, from the golden age of women's political and social work in the '70s, following the Israeli invasion and the departure from Lebanon of the PLO, lack of funds, and repression once more by the Lebanese, along with loss of hope, led to a deterioration in the social aspects of life in the camps, with many turning to religion and even the veil. Samira describes how those left behind in the camps were neglected by their leaders and her work consisted in ensuring that there was at least some support for camp families.

I am one of 11 brothers and sisters, seven girls and four boys. My father participated in the Palestinian Revolution before 1948. We left Palestine with our grandparents; my father stayed with the resistance. We first lived in Irbid, Jordan, since it is on the Lake Tiberias road. Then we moved to Damascus with my father's parents. Later, as my father had worked in an oil refinery in Haifa, we moved to Homs in Syria where he worked for the Iraqi Oil Company, IPC.

My elementary studies were in Syrian public schools. The intermediate studies were in the A'idoun camp in Homs. When Egypt and Syria were united [1958-61, a short-lived political union], Abdel Nasser visited Homs. A group of us Palestinian girls and boys met the President at the al-Saraya [government headquarters] in Homs. We designed a dark blue and white costume with a hat, on which we wrote 'Palestine' so President Abdel Nasser would recognize us among all the delegations. These were the beginnings in 1958.

Of course, before that in 1956, during the war on Port Said, we would write articles and make speeches at school. We owe much to my parents, both my mother and father, and to my teacher – her name was Inaya Wafaei – she was the one who motivated us, a very patriotic person. I do not know if she is still alive, but she was the one who formed our national identity at school. I think at the time our parents in general were open minded. We were living near the camp which was very small. All my companions in the camp were like this. There was no religious fanaticism in that period.

WOMEN'S SITUATION BEFORE THE REVOLUTION

While we were at school and participating in national activity there were no restrictions, though there were some restrictions on people ordinarily. I was in the fourth elementary class and I was chosen to make a speech against the Israeli aggression and the tripartite aggression on Egypt. We developed in this atmosphere. My mother used to wear a scarf like the Europeans; it was the same in the camps, even the peasants would wear this scarf.

My father was in the Arab National Movement (ANM). He was in the Union for Palestinian Workers at its beginning; he struggled for workers' rights. He was a member of the Administrative Committee of the General Union of Palestinian Workers. There was a struggle for workers to obtain their rights. When I had taken my baccalaureate I became an official member of the ANM. Before that we were distributing leaflets at night. 'You are a girl; this is a boy!' No, we did not have much of that. My father thought that girls should have a strong personality and they should study everything. They should be nurtured. My father had this mentality.

HUSBAND

Salah was the ANM's representative in Homs. After the defeat of 1967, we saw Salah a second time when the Fedayeen activity started and became popular, and the Arab National Movement became the Popular Front for the Liberation of Palestine – the PFLP. Of course, I was not cut off from it all even though I taught in Saudi Arabia for four years. I went with my friends who were in the movement and there we met the inspector who was Palestinian-Lebanese called Siba al-Fahoum. She was in the ANM and helped us a lot.

After the '67 war we moved from Homs to Damascus and started working with the emergency and health services. War came and the Golan was occupied by the Israelis. We were working in aid groups. In '69 I met Salah again. I was working in Damascus in the nylons factory, in accounting and business. I had left Saudi Arabia and studied in a commercial centre. Salah and I got married in 1970 and a new phase of struggle began. We married in Damascus and came directly to Lebanon. We lived in Ain al-Hilweh camp. I continued in the Popular Front and started to work with women's groups. In the beginning our work was not just for women, it also concerned the students' union. It was mixed and there was much openness. People were freed from the Lebanese authorities' oppression and, in 1969, freed from the Deuxième Bureau. [The Cairo Agreement removed the camps from the harsh jurisdiction of the Lebanese Army's intelligence services and placed them under the authority of the Palestinian Armed Struggle Command.] There was a strong Nasserite wave throughout the Palestinian camps in Lebanon after the signing of the Cairo Agreement. People were ecstatic. We started work in one area and moved on to others.

Work in PFLP and GUPW

I was chosen as a member of the General Central Committee in the PFLP, and in 1972 I was the first woman elected together with another woman from the Occupied Territory. After the second or fourth PFLP Conference, Laila Khaled and Rasmieh Awdeh joined the Central Committee. We were three, and I was made responsible for the Women's Office and the Syndical Work Committee in Lebanon.

In 1972, to resume GUPW work, I was in the Administrative Committee with Wadad Qomri, which was very active with an accumulation of experience. Then you [addressing the interviewer] came back and we worked with you. I would say that this was the golden age of women's work. There were many challenges. In general, regarding the Palestinian political organizations, each had its own women's office, but all were contributing to the Union [the GUPW]. The Union was realizing goals that women aspired to. There was also a rise in revolutionary participation. Everything follows on. The military training of women developed and women began to participate militarily — especially after the Tal al-Zaatar massacre. This phase saw a great advance in women's work; it was no longer restricted to humanitarian and charity issues. Women were beginning organized political work and more of them achieved revolutionary participation.

Women's military participation increased when the Palestinian Revolution called on all young women and university students to join. Many youngsters were trained and students came from Western and Arab universities and from Beirut University College. This started in 1978 when Israel began to strike in South Lebanon.

Our situation as Palestinians brought men and women to work together. Women had an effective role in all the Revolution's institutions, though their leadership positions did not reflect the level of their giving and struggle. But to have all these people graduate and be committed to the Revolution demonstrated their seriousness, and the GUPW fought to increase its share in the National Council and in leadership positions. The GUPW sent many women to study in the Soviet Union. The Union used to receive 30 scholarships. Palestinian women travelled and received an education abroad – in all this we accomplished something. We do not want to look just at the leadership positions. From 1973 to 1982, women's work advanced, the main reason being the national unity evident at the time. You would find in the camp's Union leadership a coordinated team from all the factions. The Union and the factions in the camps trained the cadres and raised their awareness. I remember during that period the Popular Front had a school for cadres in Shatila camp which produced many graduates. We always insisted that half the cadres be women. Other organizations would work in other places but we built a school and we brought teachers and academics specialized in Marxist political thought and philosophy. Among them were many Iraqi doctors. All the factions were sending cadres, women among them, to train in Eastern Europe. I myself went to Bulgaria for six months. Many people went to the Soviet Union for nine months. However, we felt that the local sessions were more beneficial to us as this was our reality.

Main GUPW Tasks

The Union concentrated on mobilizing and raising awareness of women and on establishing kindergartens. There was debate about syndical [trade union] and political work. There were meetings and dialogues. During the crises, those people who participated most in rescue work were the members of the Union. There was a joint Palestinian-Lebanese National Relief Committee. Lebanese and Palestinian women's work centres were opened jointly because the war was against both Palestinians and Lebanese.

The Women's Union had major cadres. Our projects were positive: a nursery for the women in the struggle and working women who had no place to keep their children; in addition, a daily kitchen – hot food for young working men and women. Umm Aouni, the cook, is still in Shatila, but older!

My Mother-in-Law

Salah was always busy and travelling due to his political commitments. Over a period of three years, our children stayed at his mother's house in Ain al-Hilweh until they went to kindergarten. This is very important. She would tell me: 'Just have more kids and don't worry!' I would reply: 'And my work?' She would say, 'It's all right, I am happy to have Salah's children here. He is the eldest and he suffered.' Thank God she saw all four of them before she died. We had a close relationship and the children would spend summer with their grandmother. I used to call her 'mother'; she was truly a wonderful mother. Salah told me that when he was in hiding and wanted to visit his parents, he would come at night through the back entrance – their house was big and they are a big family. When he got inside the house, his mother would greet him and go out. She did not trust anyone to guard the door except herself, and she would go and sit in the street until he left. She was a great lady.

Ever since I was young I had rejected a traditional marriage. I rejected anything I did not agree with. My pre-dowry was one Palestinian pound; the deferred marriage dowry was paid usually after divorce. I don't know how much dowry they provided at the time; nothing worth mentioning! We got married in Syria and at the wedding my father, without speaking to anyone or consulting Salah, when the judge marrying us asked, 'in whose hand is the bond of marriage?', immediately said: 'it is in the hands of both'. All my sisters are like that. Salah did not say anything.

WOMEN'S LIBERATION TO WHERE?

If we want to generalize, until the Israeli invasion in 1982, Palestinian women accomplished many things in Lebanon – that's assuming we leave out legal and personal status, because we are under Lebanese law in this respect, and we are refugees in their country. The struggle to change the personal status laws must be a joint one.

But some problems were not solved, like the so-called honour crimes. I remember, before 1982, a girl was cut and killed and put in the middle of the square. The girls in the Union were shocked by this incident. They met with the PLO leader Abu Ammar and demanded that the subject be tackled. But the Revolution did not interfere, and the girl was put in the middle of the square to be a lesson to others. She used to work with farmers and it seems the foreman had raped her. The socio-political situation became very harsh after the PLO withdrawal from Lebanon.

The UNRWA budget remained the same for years. Demonstrations achieved some results in order to support the Lebanon office. After Oslo the financial pumping was all inside the Occupied Territory. The Palestinian people in Lebanon suffered more than once. Even the PLO stopped supporting the people here;

the donor institutions also moved to the Occupied Territory.

As for the situation of the martyrs' families, that was even worse. If the martyr was single his family would receive 10 dollars a month and if he was married his family would receive 20 dollars a month. This was not sufficient. It was discussed at the National Council in Algeria in 1988. Abu Ammar brought me back to the Council as an Independent and I joined the Department of Refugees Affairs. We in the Palestinian delegation from Lebanon went to Tunisia with Abu Ammar. We had a session with him and laid down all issues that needed to be tackled in Lebanon. We said the first problem was the martyrs' families. The funds were increased a little, but not much. The PLO said they couldn't do more, due to the dollar exchange rate. The Palestinians in Lebanon are forbidden to work [by the Lebanese authorities].

I stayed in Lebanon after 1982. Our movement was paralyzed. The Lebanese security forces were looking for Amneh and me. They came to our homes and interrogated us, to find out if we were responsible for families and for giving them money – they wanted to know about all our activities. The PLO did not send money to anyone for a year. The Union's headquarters were taken over by the Lebanese, who confiscated everything.

If we want to speak of today's reality, we find that some women who used to be members of the different political organizations are now wearing the veil. Society has become conservative and rigid. At the beginning people were being sensitive towards the conservative reality, but this sensitivity became a way of life. Hamas does not scare us in this respect in the camps, but the drunkard who becomes a sheikh does.

When man loses hope he reverts to religion: 'Maybe God will save us'. People started like that. From 1982 to 1985 and the war of the camps [when the Palestinian camps in Lebanon came under siege], the organizations received no money. I tell you, as far as I know, the only organization that received money for its cadres was the Popular Front. Fatah started sending money for people only at the onset of the war of the camps. There was a wave of oppression, also dissidence. You cannot isolate one factor from another.

GUPW AND WOMEN'S LIBERATION

Looking back to the 1970s, this had been a marvellous phase in Lebanon when everyone was in harmony and had enlightened minds – even those we classified as right-wing wanted to show that they supported women. They feared a progressive wave, so they accepted things. It helped that there weren't any barriers. I don't imagine any union could have done more; it is the task of the Revolution, not the Union. The Union is a syndicate, and it worked: in politics, in syndicates, in supporting national unity and in different institutions its role was fantastic. It raised the name of Palestine abroad in conferences. It wouldn't be fair to blame the Union for not giving more at the time; it just wasn't possible. As for the cause of women, what the members gave, given the objective circumstances, was enough. I think we cannot underestimate the effect of wars. Each war sets us back a hundred years.

The interview was conducted in Beirut in September 2007.

11.
AMNEH KAMEL SULEIMAN (JIBREIL)

Born in 1951, father from Beit Dajan near Nablus in Palestine, Amneh currently lives in Sidon. She was a teacher with UNRWA and a child care worker with the 'Reviving the Palestinian Camp' in Lebanon. She has held many positions in the Palestinian organizations, among them and currently as member of Fatah's District Leadership and of the Higher Committee for Aid in the PLO. She is president of the Lebanon branch of the GUPW, and she has been a member of the Fatah Revolutionary Council since 1982. Amneh describes how, despite the restrictions on women and girls in society, she managed to participate in relief work in the camps in Lebanon, then in first aid and literacy projects, to become more involved politically through the Lebanese civil war, the Israeli invasion of Lebanon, the war of the camps, and up to the present day, with no regrets.

I was born in Shatila and lived there until I was 18. We were a big family of ten children. My father worked in the Gulf at the time and he would come back every two years; my mother raised and took care of us all in the early years. I would like here to salute my mother and all mothers because they all had the same role of keeping the social fabric of the family together and at the same time maintaining the Palestinian identity. It was our parents who would tell us about Palestine when we were still young. We were born in Lebanon after the uprooting. After becoming refugees and because of the atmosphere we lived in at the camp we had the motive, to a large extent, to belong to this Revolution.

I remember in 1969 when young commandos came for the first time and took over the offices of the Lebanese police in the camps.

147

They were wearing their spotted [camouflage] uniform. I was young and remember crying and feeling that something sacred had descended upon us. There was oppression and aggression in the camp [by the Lebanese intelligence service]. On many occasions they would forbid youths from standing in the street. If someone built a cement roof on their home, they would make trouble. The Deuxième Bureau worked hard and they arrested many young men who worked with the Arab National Movement.

The beginning [for me] was the meetings with students. At that time a group of Lebanese and Palestinian women supported by Fatah established Inash — the Association for the Development of Palestinian Camps (Inash Association). They established a Palestinian embroidery project and started working with Palestinian women and girls who did embroidery for a living. They also set up a library in the camp.

The GUPW in Lebanon was established in the late 1960s, but serious work began in Shatila in 1972. There were Palestinian women in the camp from different organizations. I was part of the leading committee and we concentrated on relief work, especially after the destruction of Nabatiyyeh camp [by the Israeli air force in 1974]. I remember we went as a group from the Union to remove the rubble and to contribute and distribute aid to the people. Then we were involved in abolishing illiteracy and establishing non-formal education and first aid sessions.

When the [Lebanese] civil war started we had a vital role in all the places where the Union had a presence. We would care for the wounded in the hospitals and prepare food. I remember that there were some girls who also fought in Shiyah [Beirut suburb]. Yes, we were trained; we would even be on guard in positions inside the camp.

SOCIAL CONDITIONS IN THE CAMP BEFORE THE REVOLUTION

I remember that we would go to and from school, but we were not allowed to go out, except with our parents, and we would go out all together on Sundays. Even when we went to school we were forbidden to be even one minute late, and we were allowed just to go the distance to school and back. We were not allowed out after school except to visit our female friends in the same neighborhood and were not allowed on any trip, apart from with the school, the UNRWA school. When I joined the movement, we would try to hold meetings in the daytime so we wouldn't be out late. I remember that after a while we would be late sometimes because there were activities and meetings that went on. We were scolded daily. This applied to all the girls who joined these organizations. We had to be very careful about our movements and with whom we talked. We were forbidden from entering the resistance offices because there were military people and commandos there. Meetings were held in homes until after 1976 when we began to go to the offices and talk to people. For example, I would try to help my mother in many ways to please her so she wouldn't give me trouble afterwards. I would help her with the housework so if I happened to be out late it would be alright.

I can tell you that at the beginning people and society did not view the girls who participated very positively. But after a few years the women who used to criticize us would tell us, 'Let our girls participate with you in the first aid sessions and activities in the camp'.

I gradually rose in the organization. After being a member in the Shatila division and the local committee and the area committee in the Women's Union, following the elections I became a member of the Administrative Committee. We started attracting large numbers, not only of young women but also in the field of abolishing illiteracy. We encouraged a lot of women to participate in the work. The first phase was the hardest because there was a rebellion against the existing reality and traditions, and sometimes we would challenge these.

SIEGE OF BEIRUT

Emergency Committees were formed at all levels of the GUPW: the General Secretariat, the branches, and with the Lebanese National Movement, the Lebanese Women's Groups. Social committees were formed to help the displaced wherever they were. The PLO had a big role in providing medical and health aid, and food etc. Although the bombing was by air, sea and land, we still managed to reach almost all areas: the southern suburbs, Burj al-Brajneh, and of course with Jehan [the interviewer] many times to Hayy al-Sillum to try and provide food and clothes and other needs for those who had been displaced.

SABRA AND SHATILA MASSACRE

I was with Jehan in the upper area of Abu Shaker. While we were going down flares were falling, lighting up the whole sky and ground below so the Israelis could see better to target their payload. As we walked, the flares were falling and we all thought it was the Israelis as usual lighting up the sky [so they could see where to attack]; but they were in actual fact lighting up to aid the fascist Lebanese Forces and the massacre had begun. The Lebanese Forces entered from the slope by the entrance to the Kuwaiti embassy. There were people living in Shatila who did not know that there was a massacre going on. The killing and slaughtering began not with bullets – that would have alerted people – and the houses were destroyed by bulldozers later. There were whole families such as the Sroors and Mikdadis – that family suffered the loss of 40 of its members – who were slaughtered. There were some who by chance escaped with their lives. On the third day I went with my mother, who was Lebanese. The army did not want to let us enter the camp, but we did. I saw all the dead bodies, which were covered with sheets. Nobody has the exact number of those who were massacred. I remember the Muslim Scouts and the Lebanese Red Cross were there.

People started looking for their parents and children, and because it was hot they couldn't recognize the dead bodies because most were swollen – the smell was terrible. It was said that there were about 1300 martyrs, but the Red Cross could not verify this as many people were missing and there were mass graves.

The Israelis were on the streets of Beirut and they declared a curfew. I went to Jehan in the house in Hamra where she had taken refuge, and I became very sick. I felt as though I was dying. We couldn't get hold of any medicine and Jehan made me hot drinks until morning came.

During the massacre there were people hiding in houses, many of them inside fridges, under beds and in closets. A girl and her two brothers sat in a fridge that wasn't working — there was no electricity. All life's necessities were absent and Shatila camp paid a very heavy price. There were no more than 8,000 or 10,000 people there. But that time was also a source of pride for many young men and women who worked, continued, struggled and persevered in the face of all the difficult situations.

Directly after the invasion many people were lost because of the behaviour of the army and the massacre. People did not know where their children were. We cooperated with the Committee of Lebanese Prisoners and Missing People. There was also the Committee for the Arrested; it was formed in 1976 with Widad Halwani and a large group. We prepared lists of missing people and worked on them. We made many visits to the prime minister, the Parliament, the UN, to human rights institutions, embassies and newspapers. Even now there are people whose fate is still unknown, whether they are dead or alive.

WAR OF THE CAMPS AND THE UNITY OF THE GUPW [1985-88]

There were great challenges, especially after the Israeli invasion. We in the GUPW tried as much as possible to avoid political differences. We worked, all the factions in the Union worked, because we really felt that we were facing a social catastrophe which required unified efforts to decrease the suffering of our people in the camps. We continued even after the schism inside Fatah because the base and the cadres who worked on the ground were in harmony and understood each other. In this way we avoided many problems, especially during the war of the camps, and we continued to help our people.

Some attempted to make me leave Shatila during the war of the camps, in the sense that I was greatly fatigued and had worked constantly. But I told them that my fate was the same as our people, and it was impossible to leave the camp. There were mothers like Umm Abed Aantar, Umm Mohammad and Umm Kamal Harb, each of whom had lost four of her family – young men – as well as Umm Mohammad Afifi. I could not leave those who had lost their young men.

I made a decision in the end: I either die with these people or leave with them. That's why I stayed in the camp with many sisters and brothers till the last minute, until it fell. I am proud of this experience, although it was bitter, but I consider that the women in the camp were a guarantee against many collisions among the factions. When there was an alert between any two organizations we would seek the help of women. They would organize a demonstration and go to the groups' offices: 'Beware of doing anything, this is our camp and these are our people and our children here and nobody is allowed to disrupt matters. He who has no family here cannot fire one shot in the camp.' In this way we prevented many fights. I always say that these women, who are the mothers of the martyrs, are the unknown soldiers. These women provided food for the camp, gasoline for the hospital, medicines, clothes, and sometimes money, as it was forbidden for anyone to leave the camp. Many of the women who did move around were taken prisoner and tortured by the Syrians and Amal militia. Regrettably, many of them suffered and still have health problems.

Many of the girls who used to take goods into the camps suffered from problems with their kidneys, skin or bodies, and those who carried the food, among them Jamila, Nadwa and Um Ihsan, each had a role in the perseverance of the camp. I did not forget that every time a young man was martyred a baby would be born in his place! During the siege 40 babies were born — imagine the dilemma. We would provide some butter and food so that the woman could breastfeed her child. We would gather items from the destroyed houses around the camp and provide food for people. There were many marriages in the camp during the battle. Seriously, this was a dilemma for the Palestinian people: when a young man would fall martyr, two or three days later another would get married, hanging on to life and continuity. No one expected to come out alive from the camp. In spite of the bitterness of this experience it strengthened social relations between people. We remained in contact with these young men and women, as well as older women who were in the camp, despite the many differences and political disagreements.

WOMEN'S LIBERATION

Many women started to rebel. Some women were subjected to violence and beatings. Women became strong. They would no longer accept oppression, especially if they were economically independent. Experience proved that the more economically independent a woman is the more likely she is to overcome large obstacles and be able to decide for herself. Although women reached some leadership positions, we cannot say that they

153

contributed to decision making, sometimes they could not even make their own decisions; but now the situation is better than before.

SOCIAL TRANSFORMATION AND SOCIAL ISSUES

As for social problems and family differences, the complainants would go first to the family elders who were from the same village in Palestine. If the problem was solved, all well and good, if not, they would turn to the influential people in the camp, and sometimes the Popular Committee, or raise the matter at the regional level or with Abu Ammar, God rest his soul. Many issues were raised.

The Revolution came and gathered a momentum, which led to a very big change in our lives as Palestinians. In my opinion, when the Resistance was there, people did not worry about anything. I would not hear about someone who needed help for an open heart operation, because the PLO covered the cost for Palestinians and Lebanese. The Palestinian Red Crescent covered health needs of the Palestinian people. There were resources, but after 1982 there was a catastrophe. After the invasion, and when the Resistance left, there was huge unemployment, as the PLO and its various institutions had absorbed a large number of Palestinians in Lebanon. It was offering health services, infrastructure for the camps, and social assistance as well as providing for martyrs families. All this dwindled after 1982.

This Palestinian leadership did not take the issue of women seriously. There was no special programme for women and their representation was not clear or serious in the Revolution's institutions or in the leadership positions. Women participated in all the battles and in all phases of the struggle. However, practically speaking and until now the Palestinian woman has still not taken up her right of representation and decision-making. She fell martyr, she fought, she participated in military operations and in social and political fields and elsewhere; but practically, until now, the Palestinian leadership has demonstrated no serious view regarding women.

The camp integrated into the body of the Revolution, the camp was the reservoir of the Revolution. But the problem was that we emerged from one war to face another. When the Israeli invasion occurred, we said a catastrophe, a disaster or an earthquake has hit us. Then the war of the camps occurred and we forgot the invasion. You know how. Every time something happens you forget the thing before it, even though it is very bitter, cruel and hard. This is our life. Our generation saw not one nice day!

What are the dimensions of this situation? The Palestinian in Lebanon lives in a constant state of anxiety, unable to work or travel normally. Our very lives are threatened – that's why we are always worried. I refer to the diseases that are afflicting Palestinians now. You know that most people here have diabetes and high blood pressure; even the girls who work in the Union, even children have high blood pressure and diabetes.

WE SUCCEEDED IN FACING THE CHALLENGE

I consider that my first awareness, growing up and maturation was within the framework of the Union. I also consider that we had aware and responsible people in the leadership of the Union. This experience affected us a lot. The continuation of our work until now, despite all the difficult and complicated circumstances, is due to our strong roots, for me and many of the cadres in the Fatah movement and the Women's Union. The civil war came, the Israeli invasion came, then the war of the camps; all the wars were a challenge for us, and I believe that we succeeded in facing the challenge because we carried on, despite all the difficult circumstances.

I think that the centres and projects we built until now are proof of the right path we were raised on from the beginning. We really worked with the conviction and faith that our cause was just and that we should mobilize all efforts to attain our rights. I think that this correct build-up contributed a lot to the continuity of our work within the framework of the Union. The Union's achievements in Lebanon are proof of this build-up, as the Israeli invasion destroyed all we had achieved since the 1970s. But we were able to establish something new. All these projects we are working on in kindergartens, career qualifications, loans, treatment, psychological and social interventions, building and enabling the cadres – all are proof of the right foundation.

I did not choose not to marry; I am a woman like all women who would like to settle down and live amongst a family and build her life normally. No one chooses not to marry but some people face difficult circumstances, maybe barriers that prevent them from settling down. I am like many of my sisters, whose fate did not help them, nor the circumstances lived by the Palestinians in general in relation to their movement and identity. I once had a relationship which might have ended in marriage but the obstacle was that I couldn't get a visa. The young man and I agreed to continue our education abroad. We got engaged, and then he travelled hoping I would follow. I tried many times, but after a while the Israeli invasion came with all its consequences and hardships. After a while, I tried to get a visa to America but as a Palestinian refugee I was unable to do so. I did not get the visa and the relationship ended. He couldn't come to me because of his passport.

The inhuman circumstances we lived through as Palestinians interfered with the minute details of our lives. I was like many others whose families were scattered in different countries by the difficult circumstances. After 23 years, my family was reunited with my brothers and my father, God rest his soul.

I became increasingly involved in the struggle, and it became too late to think of anything else. Work took all my time and concerns. I have no regrets. On the contrary, I think that when I am working and serving our people and solving some problems along with my sisters, this enriches my life as a Palestinian human being. Just like many female Palestinian activists who really forgot their own lives when their main concern was the cause and its people.

Today is Mother's Day. On Mother's Day I feel I am a mother to many people. I have an inner richness because of people's love for us. I think everything has a price in this world: when we choose this path, and are convinced of it, we have to bear all its consequences. Of course, I am like many other Palestinian women who are still struggling until now.

The interview was conducted in two phases: the first in Sidon, September 2007, and the second in Beirut, March 2008.

Military training, 1980

12.
ROUND TABLE DISCUSSION

*Some cadres of the General Union of Palestinian Women (GUPW)
participated in a round table discussion in Ain al-Hilweh camp,
Sidon. They included several women based in South Lebanon who
didn't give their names. Other participants included **Amneh
Suleiman**, President of GUPW – Lebanon branch; **Amal
Mohammad** (Um Sari), former kindergarten supervisor; **Amal
Shehabi**, public health professional and formerly GUPW
kindergartens supervisor; **Raja' Shbayta** (Umm Amer), social
worker; **Basma Antar**, Director of Karama Institute for Disabled
Palestinians and responsible for the literacy campaign in Miyyeh
wa Miyyeh; **Zakiyye Hassanein**, former employee of the Council
of Churches Joint Christian Committee (JCC) and careers advisor;
Alia Abdallah (Umm Yasser), kindergarten teacher and
responsible for the Huda Shaalan Palestinian Heritage Institute;
Kananah Rahmeh, Secretary of GUPW in Miyyeh wa Miyyeh and
currently in Sidon; **Thurayya Mohammad**, archives administrator
of the Popular Struggle Front and member of GUPW
Administrative Committee in Lebanon; **Amina Saleh** Urasan,
Secretary of GUPW in Miyyeh wa Miyyeh and social worker.*

Jehan Helou: I am happy today to meet a group of active women
from the General Union of Palestinian Women – Lebanon branch
to talk about their personal experiences in the struggle in South
Lebanon during and after the Israeli occupation, and to share points
of view regarding the situation of women.

Um Sari: From my point of view as a Palestinian woman I think our situation is a political one; we were raised in a political society, among political families whose daily bread was news and politics. Our parents left Palestine, so we lived the Palestinian cause day and night, accustomed to the stories they would tell us of what they underwent when they left and of the first period of becoming refugees.

My first political experience was during the Israeli invasion of Lebanon in 1982. I was a student at school, but when the invasion came and schools closed I felt that as a Palestinian girl I had another, different situation, other than what we read about in books: there was the problem of a whole people. I started to educate myself. I read a lot, and later was introduced to the idea of a kindergarten run by the Women's Union; so I decided to become a member and find out what was going on there, and what Palestinian women were doing. First of all I spoke with my mother about joining. But my mother said 'No, your brother was martyred in the invasion, and I wouldn't want to bear two wounds, one after the other. And you are still so young.'

In response I did not eat for three days. I am the youngest at home, so my mother gave in and told me: 'do whatever you want'. And thus I began. On entering the kindergarten I found that the issue was not merely one of children and kindergartens; that there were no young men, only women and children and that their suffering was great. The women started going to other institutes, asking for help from them and for UNRWA aid and food cartons. I felt that we needed to lift women out of their situation: why should women just be mothers with children? Why, for example, shouldn't we demand that the prisoners be freed? And so we started going to houses in the camp asking the women to join us in a demonstration directed at the Israeli military governor to demand the freeing of prisoners from Ansar [detention camp run by the Israeli military in South Lebanon]. The older women said: 'What, these kids are going to lead us?'

At first we gathered together as students, but then all the parents of the prisoners came and I was surprised to see my mother standing with the other women, although at that time we ourselves did not have a prisoner in Ansar; and we led the demonstration from the camp to the door of the military governor. Its result was the release of those under 60, or between 50 and 60, and then of the young men of 14, 15 and 16.

But then we were surprised by a big conspiracy against the camp. There would be a knock at the door and the residents would be told: 'Defence Army [Israel Defence Forces] — open up'. People would open their doors and the first person to open the door would be killed. This was repeated four or five times. In response the Israelis increased their patrols; then they said, 'We want to sit with those who represent the camp'. I was greatly surprised when some of the older people came and asked me to join them in the meeting with the Israelis. They did not want to sit with the men alone and they wanted new blood to talk: 'You young people are still beginning, it is important your voices be heard!' And we were keen to join them. The Israelis told us they couldn't protect every house from what was happening.

For sure, they were Lebanese forces or Antoine Lahd's forces [Antoine Lahd was head of the South Lebanon Army which was allied to the Israeli forces] who were doing the killing. They would knock on the door and say 'Defence Army'. At our meeting the Israelis said: 'We cannot put a soldier outside each door, but what we can do is arm you; we will give you weapons for you to protect yourselves with'. Here the men were anxious that maybe now they would take us to Ansar; we looked at one another and took a moment to think, and after a moment's consultation I suddenly found myself speaking and telling the Israelis, 'What does this mean? That we will become a second Lahd?' So everyone was encouraged to reject the proposal. However, we carried out a sort of self-arming: this one has a rifle, that one a gun, and we had guards at night. In this women also had a role.

The situation imposed itself. My husband understood my need for this work. We opened a new kindergarten that I was in charge of. Then there was the Amal movement [Lebanese Shiite organization], which brought its own worries. I had my first child by then. I was summoned [for questioning] by Amal, and they entered and searched the house after I had left. I liked to read a lot and had a book of Marxist philosophy, which they discovered. My family and myself, along with my father-in-law's family, were all living together in the same house. Amal set fire to the house, starting with the kitchen. Luckily, our neighbours, with whom we had good relations, were Shiites, and prevented Amal's forces from destroying the house. They began to extinguish the fire and only the kitchen was burned.

These were difficult times with much suffering. There was no stability. I stopped my activities for a little while because of the security situation, and I was unable to find a house in an area where there was political cover for us. But when the first opportunity arose, I returned to my activities.

Amal: *Amal Shehabi, Education Supervisor in the General Union of Palestinian Women in Sidon.* I have been involved in politics since I was young. I was in the camp for Ashbal/Zahrat [scouts and guides] where children were taught the history and geography of Palestine. I was raised in a house where patriotism prevailed; my brother is younger than me but he was with Ashbal and he encouraged me. I did not experience the difficulties you speak of – this was before all that. There would be training at the level of the schools, the schools of UNRWA.

Before the invasion there was compulsory military service, which I joined. We trained on mortars and the quadruple [machine gun]. For a while – until the invasion – we would look after the checkpoints. I was at the end of my first year at school in Sibleen.

We did not expect to see the Israeli army among us; but two days after the invasion they had reached Sidon and we saw the tanks. It took a month for Ain al-Hilweh camp to fall and they were able to enter. There were eleven young men who fought to the end inside the camp. At that time there was definitely a big role for women because they were the only ones who were able to move about; they were able to go and get the salaries for the men and their families. If the young man was head of the family and a prisoner in Ansar, the woman would take the initiative; she would bring the salaries from the PLO in Damascus for her son, for her husband and for many families. This was risky.

At that time I was ready to do something. I remember the first incident that happened with me was when the Israelis gathered together all the young men in Ain al-Hilweh following the fall of the camp. They gathered the men from age 14 to 60. My father was among them, and one of my little brothers. I also had a missing brother – we didn't know where he was – and an uncle who was wounded and had been taken prisoner. Half the young men in our household had disappeared. I was standing among the women who were waiting to see if their men would return. They gathered at the government hospital. One of the Israeli soldiers was standing in front of me and winking, and every time I turned my face he would do like that [Amal makes a gesture]. Finally I told him: 'Shame on you, son of a....!' So he grabbed me by the shoulder and hit me – it hurt for a week. This honestly scared my parents a lot. The neighbours warned my mother that I would be arrested. So I started sleeping each day in a different place. My mother said: 'Isn't it enough what's happened to your brothers – now you!' So she made me escape to Tripoli and thence to Syria. I stayed in Syria unwillingly until the Sibleen School re-opened. Then my mother came and told me I should go back to school.

And so I returned. I have a brother who was in the Fatah movement who told me, 'We need you to do something.' 'I asked what it was. He said you have to get us a few things – some weapons and maps for some of the brothers who are here inside the camp. So I went to Bekaa with my mother. At the time the road was cut off – it was February – so one of the Fatah officials told me, 'since you are here, let me train you a bit'. I said okay. So we began some weapons training. He told me, 'If you want to do something useful, take these maps for me,' and so I did. I was keen to help.

When I came back home I was surprised to find there was no organization, nowhere to go except to Hajja Alia – one of the sisters who has her own history of struggle – of course she would direct us! We were honestly motivated but without seriously thinking what we were doing. We wanted to do something, but what? I would tell Ahmad, her brother's friend and ours, that I wanted to throw a bomb, or something; he would say 'No, Amal, you have to calm down, you must plan correctly.' Then there was a teacher in Sibleen who taught health and told me he had received a letter from the Bekaa that I was from Fatah and willing to work. I asked him what was required. He said, 'You must work with me, but silently: you cannot ask me questions, neither about what organization is involved, nor who is with you, nor who it is you are communicating with, or anything.' I told him I was ready.

And so along with a couple of other girls we travelled around the south, smartly dressed, with forged identity cards bearing an Israeli stamp, sometimes with weapons in the car.

Eventually, Mr. A. was killed in an operation by the Israelis, and the army came and arrested me and the other girls. Five of us were captured – it was not easy for the parents. When I got out of prison I found my mother had been unable to bear the strain. Her tears never dried; the neighbours came constantly to console her. They were all worried about what might be happening to me inside, and imagining the worst.

We suffered most in the Israeli quarters where we stayed for almost ten days; the torture was psychological. I was captured in the morning; but then they entered the house at night and took my brother, because I worked with him, and it hadn't been long since he had been released. They threatened me saying they would bring my brother and do with me so and so in front of him. They put Amneh in one room and me in another, I did not know that she had been captured and she did not know that I had been captured. I refused to talk and so did Amneh. They tried to lure us, until I stayed for three days in the corner of a room with a bag over my head, which they would remove whenever they wanted to question me. After a week I had a nervous breakdown; they would drag me and carry me from room to room where there was questioning. I remember there was a doctor who would put needles into me – I would pass out and wake up to find the needle stuck in me and blood everywhere. In the end I reached a phase where I was neither eating nor drinking. When I wanted to go to the toilet two would accompany me, so how could I do it? I refused food and drink so that I wouldn't need to go to the toilet, and reached a phase where I collapsed. When I had fits they put me in with the young women, who when they saw me covered in blood screamed in horror.

We suffered a lot until they took us to the women's prison. When we entered and saw our former school principal and others there whom we knew, the sisters warmly embraced us. My father was there. Many embraced me, though it was unpleasant when you heard people saying, 'How many men touched her?' However, there was no sexual assault though there was the threat of it, and we lived in a terrified psychological state. But they had used this method with girls before us, girls who were older than us, or with older women – when they used very dirty methods. Our reception by society was very good on the whole and they made me forget all the suffering; it was only a very small minority who were unpleasant. Even my parents were understanding and my grandfather, who is an old man, would say, 'My granddaughter!' I would tell him, 'Grandfather, raise your head, thank God I wasn't an Israeli agent!' Imagine, when the Israelis came to take me he wouldn't let me go with them in the jeep, saying, 'You are forbidden to go with them or I will kill you!' When the Israelis said, 'She must come with us,' he said, 'No, I will take her. You want to take her to the military quarters? I will take her and it shan't be said that my son's daughter is an Israeli agent. I don't want her to go with you in the jeep, because he who sees her passing by will say she is collaborating with the Israelis.' So, imagine, he, my grandfather, drove me to the government headquarters in his own car!

One of the sisters: All our Palestinian people began their political activity as a result of the persecution they lived through. There were those who lived the persecution in Palestine and left; we lived the persecution in the camps. Our father was persecuted by the Deuxieme Bureau. Maybe that was something that strongly motivated me to join in activities against them. There were four young men in Ain al-Hilweh camp before the arrival of the Revolution here who used to work with the Arab nationalists, military work against Israel. As they had returned from occupied Palestine, the Deuxieme Bureau killed them. They then forbade their parents to bury them in a cemetery. So these four were buried in the house; there was a hole in the bathroom, and that is where they were buried. It was forbidden to bury them outside the camp. Many others were similarly killed.

Amneh: This is our history. When the explosion at the PLO Research Centre happened [1983] I was there for a meeting of the aid committee. I said, 'Where is Salah Salah? Why is he late?' In fact they were all late for the meeting. After a while I said, 'If they're not coming we must leave, because we have work'. I went down to the library on the floor below where my sister Jamileh worked. She was wearing pink and had fixed her hair, so I told her, 'You look like a bride today'. Cheese had been put out for breakfast, and I was about to help myself when Jamileh told me, 'Sister, please leave the Centre'. When I asked her why she said, 'If we both die my mother will go crazy. Just go'. So I got in the car and when I reached Rawsheh I heard an explosion. I arrived at the Union building; unaware the explosion was at the Centre. At the Union building, on Corniche al-Mazraa, everyone was coming out and we were told to evacuate the area. Someone said to me: 'Don't you know the Research Centre has collapsed?' I became crazy and when one of the French soldiers [from the multinational forces] tried to calm me, I hit him. Then I saw my brother with his wife, and he told me, 'We can't find Jamileh'. So we went to the hospital and found her sitting in a chair, her hair all torn out. A woman who had been with her was dead – she had only just become engaged that very day!

The main motive for women's involvement in the beginning was a patriotic one. Following the invasion we felt that there was catastrophe at every level. The Israelis destroyed houses, wounded and killed people, and imprisoned 14-year old children in Ansar.

There weren't many men around, which is why the foreign press when they interviewed us would say: 'The South is the kingdom of women'. Here was the biggest role for Palestinian women in rebuilding their lives, because Ain al-Helweh camp – the largest in Lebanon – was like a football pitch after the invasion, totally flattened. Those who rebuilt it were the women and children.

Raja' Moussa Shabayta (Umm Amer): We are from the southern area of Ain al-Hilweh camp and were targeted by the Israeli bombardment, as well as during the war of the Phalangist and other attacks. We remained in the shelters for 21 days during the invasion of 1982, and when we emerged we found our houses had been partly destroyed. The first area where clearance and reconstruction started was our own. Of course there were weapons in every house and those we found we would store away. The Phalangist cleared our houses and told us we were forbidden to live there anymore and that the land had an owner and he wanted it back.

UNRWA began to set us up with tents, dividing the land according to each family. But we women rejected this and banded together to burn the tents with gasoline. There were no men at all, only boys of 13 and younger. We built the houses with our own hands. This was the first women's uprising inside the camp.

Our area was close to Darb al-Seem – an area full of Phalangist. During the invasion the Phalangist began to infiltrate the camp. The first person they killed was Abu Mansour from Safouri. They would come in patrols with the aim of taking over the camp. We women demonstrated with a march from the camp to the Israeli military quarters, which they had set up in the government offices in Sidon. We demanded that the Israelis patrol the area to protect us from the Phalangist, since it was the Israelis who had taken our men to Ansar, leaving the women and children alone. And so they had to establish positions and patrols day and night. This was in August 1982.

Zakiyye Hassanein: Of course each of us has her own experience. I am from the Popular Front but, with respect to my organization, I am always proud to say that I am in the Women's Union [GUPW].

During the invasion of 1982, I lived outside the camp in the neighbourhood of Sidon and I had a brown-coloured card from the General Union of Palestinian Women, which I had mislaid. I joined the Union through my sister Samira who had joined before me. I would search the house daily for about a week. I would say to Samira, 'I don't know where my Union card is'. She would say, 'Forget it'. One day the Israelis came and captured some men from the area ... I asked Samira: 'What about our area?' She told me, 'They will leave it to the end'. 'I'm not scared for myself,' I told

Samira. 'If they come and ask for you, don't give yourself up, and if they ask for me I will give myself up; you should leave in any case.'

One day they came early. All the women and children were out of the houses. But in our house there was my brother's wife, God rest her soul, and some small children and an old woman. They took all the men. I was sitting on a cloak in the road and witnessed Abu al-Abed and Naji al-Ali [the famous Palestinian caricaturist] being beaten and I saw the tanks and the masked men. There was a tank next to me carrying Israeli soldiers, but I did not know that it had stopped for me. Once they had taken all the men, they came for me. I have a brother who was made to stand aside. All the men of the neighbourhood who were in the police and the municipality were standing and I was sitting. One of the Israeli soldiers came up to me and said, 'You are Zakiyye'. 'How do you know?' I asked. 'This is your Union card,' he said. He opened it; my picture and name were there, so there was no point in denying it. He asked me what the card was for. I told him, 'Sewing is what's written on it; I work in sewing and I have the right to be in the syndicate of tailors'. He asked me, 'Where is your house?' I told him: 'This is it'. He said 'We want to blow it up'. So I replied, 'Listen, if you want to blow it up, go ahead, but it is against the law; there are children and an old woman and orphans inside. Get the people who are in the house out, then blow it up.' He told me to go with him. I walked in front of him not knowing if the weapons were pointed at my back. My concern was to make my sister understand that I was the one they were asking for. I took one step and with the other I reached the stairs; I lifted up the cloak and took three steps forward: 'Samira, it is me not you, get out of the house,' and I stopped. The soldier said go and change your clothes and come with us. I took off my clothes and put on cowboy trousers and a shirt. They searched the house – and that was a terrible moment. They mixed the clothes up with the food and suchlike. They took me to the square where we came across my mother carrying food and she told me 'Come on, my dear, why are you standing here? Come home – what do you want with them?' I told her to go to the house and that I would follow. So she did – she knew that they wanted to arrest me. You should see what happened to her!

They took me to the square and the officers started questioning me: 'What is your work? Who are your friends? What books do you read? Who visits you?' All this was in the square with people standing around. But the one nice thing that I won't forget was that the young men of the neighbourhood, and the mayor, Hussein Moussa, and the president of the municipality, all of them Lebanese, came to the square and told the Israelis, 'Take us instead and leave this girl; we raised her and we will not allow you to take her.'

There was a four or five-hour interrogation under the sun – it was exhausting. I sat on the ground; they finally left, telling me, 'Go home and let us know about any terrorist who comes to the house'. This did not make me sit at home; on the contrary, they had already taken Nabila, Amal and Abla. Now, God strengthen him, Abu Maher al-Yamani sent me a letter: Let your sister leave and you remain. I stayed and we worked in secret, which gave us strength. The men were in prison. We all worked, I give credit to all; we worked under the care of the wives of our prisoners, of our martyrs, and with the aid that came from Damascus and the Bekaa; how we delivered it, how we tied thread to thread, we followed the way of the occupied land. We did not know one another, yet we mobilized Lebanese people with us; they would go to the Bekaa and bring what we needed in an organized manner. How did we react when an Israeli patrol passed by? How did we keep watch?

There was further destruction of houses. Two or three families would live closely, cooking and eating together. How the Palestinian women here worked, carrying and moving sand from one place to another! The journey of Palestinian women is very, very rich.

Amneh: In 1982, I came here. I was told to pretend to be mute so we could pass through the checkpoint. One of Saad Haddad's group [South Lebanon Army established by Israel] asked me at the checkpoint: 'Where are you from?' I put my hand over my mouth and didn't answer, and so we arrived at the camp. We all worked in the fields. We managed to be in constant communication. I, for example, was in Beirut at a certain period, and Kanana and Alia were here, but we were in touch; during the sieges and battles we would communicate through letters. There were many problems and everyone was committed to work – except one [laugh]. We worked together; there was continuity. Kanana, Alia, Zahra, Fayzeh – in the most difficult times during battles and the security situation, we could not move from camp to camp; the work between us would be done by letter and phone. We wanted to serve in whatever way was possible. Even within the Union, for example, we would try to prevent some members from being exposed or their affiliation declared so that the work could proceed. I think that honesty and high ethics played a very big role in our success – we never stopped working, although the situation was complicated and difficult.

Following the Israeli invasion, we developed a lot in our work. Our centres were very small and not reinforced with concrete, which was scary; the situation was very bad, but we continued to build our centres. Our institutes, the kindergartens – we built them all. We put our lives into this Union, efforts, strength and youth. The Union carried out many projects and remained here.

Alia Abdallah: Our experience started when we were young; our parents would talk to us about Palestine and their parents: some of them had stayed inside and some left. My father was in the Arab Nationalist Movement. The Hajja, my mother, sold her braids and bought a rifle before 1948. This showed the mentality and extent

171

of patriotic feelings. My maternal uncle was involved in secret activities; my cousin became a martyr in the battle of Salt. That's how we lived. Then came the events of 23 April 1969 [a day of confrontation between the Palestinian and Lebanese demonstrators and the Lebanese army] and we were among the pioneers in the demonstration. I was 18 years old.

I went from Ain al-Hilweh to Sidon. There were demonstrations in Ain al-Hilweh and Rashidiyeh camps. Here in Sidon also there was shooting. The Lebanese minister of defence ordered soldiers to open fire on the demonstrators should they reach Sidon. We marched from the government quarters to Martyrs' Square. The army began firing on the young men, and they shot the first one who was carrying the Palestinian flag; he fell to the ground, so the second one came and took up the flag, and then the third, who was also hit. We entered from the Ruwwas station, and the owner of the building appeared, telling us to get out. I retorted, 'We may die, but we will not be humiliated!' And so we continued to the Sidon municipality building. When we reached Sidon, the army came and closed the entrances to the camp, so people could neither get in nor out.

My uncle's wife found me and said, 'Come along, don't go home – I will take you to my parents and we will wait till things calm down'. At home, when it was close to sunset, it was feared that Alia had fallen a martyr, as she was nowhere to be seen; they checked at the governmental hospital and when I arrived home I found the entrance to the house had become a place of lamentation. 'Where have you been? God help you, you almost killed us!' I explained I had been at my uncle's house. This was how it all began.

Then came the organized work and initiatives. The first organized meeting was in 1970 in Ain al-Hilweh with both men and women present. Of course, before you go to the meeting you feel it is something very big and you don't want to tell anyone or say what happened there. But then I tried to politicize and organize the girls.

My parents are patriotic. My father was in the Popular Front and the rest of our family was in Fatah. There was a conflict. My brother was born in 1970. I wanted to name him Yasser after Yasser Arafat; my father would not accept this, so we cast a lot and Yasser won. Father called him Thaer for a while, but later he did call him Yasser! My mother was an independent member of the Union. But when I wanted to go I would first of all do the housework and prepare everything for her and then get ready myself. Mother would ask me, 'Where are you off to?' and I would answer: 'Just for half an hour'. It is true that we could go out, but we followed tradition, with no visits here, there and everywhere. If we went to a meeting it meant only the meeting and then we would come straight home. If I was going to see Amneh, it meant one hour and I would return. Honesty in dealing with parents and society made society encourage and support women.

I was in a very harmonious group in Ain al-Hilweh – just as we are now. After me, one of the brothers would come from time to time and give a talk, and if there was a martyr, for example, we would attend his funeral. In 1973 came the first shelling of the camp. We were members of Fatah. Najat was the one responsible for the women. She was in the Fatah leadership division in the camp.

One of the women: Unfortunately, the social conditions were such that many were in need of social security support. After the withdrawal of the PLO in 1982, the social conditions [in the camp] deteriorated.

One of the women: We were thinking of starting a home for the elderly. Even we ourselves, who did all this, where would we go? We have tragedies. When people were struggling, no one knew that they would come out of all this with nothing. Not only the unmarried, but also the married ones, might not have children to care for them, or their children would emigrate, or their circumstances would be problematic.

Alia: In this period in the 1970s we did first-aid courses. There were around thirty-five volunteers in the camp. When the Syrians came in 1976 [the Syrians intervened in the Lebanese civil war of in 1976] we were in a state of mobilization. The Women's Union formed committees and took over shelters in the Ta'meer area, next to the camp, encouraging people to use them, then followed up on their needs there, for example, if they were sick or had other requirements.

After this period, I entered the military and worked with the radio. There were 12 of us women and we had to sleep two days away from home and return the following day. My brother was travelling at the time, and when he came back he asked my mother where I was. He himself was connected to the struggle but he did not expect me to join the military and stay away from home. But I talked to him about it, and it was okay. We were in the first artillery division, the radio being part of the artillery school. We continued to work in the organization until the Israeli invasion of 1982. Before '82 there was some shelling and I went to aid the injured but got caught up in it. In fact I was declared dead three times by the Democratic Front, because it was their base that was hit. I was hit. After the invasion we opened a kindergarten while still under Israeli occupation. My sister was captured, but I escaped.

Others: It was during Israel's presence that the Phalangist were active on the ground. Samir Geagea's war started [Samir Geagea was a Lebanese warlord later imprisoned for crimes he had committed].

WOMEN'S PARTICIPATION ESCALATED

One of the women: Before 1982 there weren't many women involved in patriotic activity. After '82 there were many more. They were driven by the experience of the Israeli occupation and the arrest of people at Ansar. The arrests were indiscriminate – those involved and those not involved; so the people who were not involved, and yet were arrested, had more motivation to join the resistance.

Another woman: These days things are changing. Before, there was organizational education. I remember when we got involved in the struggle, we did not care to take salaries – in fact we would pay to participate. Now it is very different; participation in the resistance has become a job, to answer a material and economic need. But when we started off it was very different – there was struggle. That's why the original group exists no longer; and though we still try to speak of our experiences, in reality we do not talk about the rich experience we lived. Such discussion as we are having now should be documented so that it will be known and studied from one generation to the next. The beginning was different in our days. Each one of us joined the struggle from her conviction; she would overcome her parents' objections and challenge society. Nowadays a father might request work for his daughter; it has become a material need.

Another interjects: Before, our parents were economically responsible for us; now they are dying of hunger. The economic situation is more pressured than before.

Alia: If any untoward event happens nowadays you find people gathering up their things and leaving; whereas before you would think: what can I do to help people to stay. For example, I was a contact point for the whole area and would be asked whether people should go or stay – how safe was it? If they were to stay we had to provide for their needs, if they wanted to leave we had to check whether it was safe or not. Now no one bears responsibility for anyone.

Amneh: Do you remember, Jehan, in 1973 when we went to Nabatiyyeh after the camp was bombarded by Israel? We went to remove the rubble, to try and persuade people to come back; and during the Israeli invasion in 1978 we went to Burj al-Shimali to help people remove the rubble and clean the streets so as to reinforce the camp during the war of the camps, and [the same thing] during the invasion of 1982. At the time we worked through the Women's Union and its different committees. We would be in the hospitals, preparing food, in the different quarters, collecting blood, distributing food, making sure the buildings where the refugees were displaced were clean and free of scabies, providing medicine and necessities. There was the PLO, Fatah and all the Palestinian leadership – you felt you had their support and protection everywhere.

Now [after the PLO and the resistance had left Lebanon], who will protect us in the camps? It is true that there is a PLO presence, but not a strong one that would, for example, enable us to face battles such as took place in Nahr al-Bared, where people left because there was no force to protect them when a terrorist group settled in the camp, and the camp was destroyed. The people there didn't feel that the battle [with the Lebanese Army] was truly their battle.

Kananah Rahmeh (Miyye wa Miyye camp). Maybe we were among the first people in the camp to join the resistance, the first two girls, me and Zeinab Rabbani. We didn't have any problems at home, within the family; our problems were more within camp society. Of course, society was conservative. But I had no problem at home. My mother, God rest her soul, had died; my father was there, he would encourage me to go out – and the same with Zeinab. But would Palestinian camp society accept a girl going out of the house alone? No, they wouldn't. But we had a vision, and we tried to make our behaviour suitable for our society and our camp so we would not be a bad influence on the next generation. We did not want to encourage negative reactions. We worked in many fields. We joined the Palestinian Women's Union and were on the local committee.

Basma Antar (Miyye w Miyye camp) Kananeh is talking about conservatism in behaviour. We would try to keep our behaviour conservative, why? Because, at the beginning, no girl would dare do anything because people were very fanatical and it was the first time a girl was wearing trousers, military trousers, and going to train with men, carrying weapons, running round the track and jumping over fire. Many parents forbade their daughters from taking part in these areas.

Kananah: No, I pointed out two aspects: the home and society. We did not have opposition from home, but we did not have the backing of society. That's why we did not go directly into training. We were cautious about this.

I came up gradually in the organization of Fatah; we would have organizational sessions, even reading the internal constitution, reciting the ten points. Then we rose gradually in the Palestinian Women's Union; we were in the local unit. The kindergarten was opened and that was our initial work; we also worked at erasing illiteracy. We would bring women from their homes and if the woman was working, we would go to the house and help her with her work so that she could come to the literacy class. But then came the invasion of 1982.

177

ERASING ILLITERACY

Kananah: It was 100 per cent successful.

Amneh: In 1982 we had a programme to erase illiteracy in Shatila camp. Women of all ages from 28 to 45 came. Umm Khaled was among them. There were 13 women. We held classes three days a week in the afternoons. Umm Khaled was with us while her husband was in Abu Dhabi; every time he sent her a cheque she had to go and cash it, which required her to sign at the bank. She didn't know how to sign, so she would leave a fingerprint. She told me: 'When I put my fingerprint, I am very sad because everyone signs and writes except me.' After three months she could write her name and was able to sign at the bank. She said she felt in another world when she read the newspaper, like a new human being. The women continued the classes until they could read and write, and I haven't forgotten them till now.

Kananah: The most important thing is that they read the Quran and the newspapers, and some would follow up on their children at school. We accomplished a lot in erasing illiteracy. If a woman was absent we would try to find out why that was; if she was sick we would visit her.

In 1979 I joined a training course in the Soviet Union and it was a big leap forward. My father, God rest his soul, was at home and I was responsible for my siblings; but you have to go and see another world! Umm Omar (Jehan) was behind all that. The course in Russia was very good; it was a chance to see other peoples, to live with them. I remember both its negative and positive aspects. After we returned we continued in the kindergarten – and then came the invasion of 1982.

The invasion was a surprise to us; we had no experience. But necessity is the mother of invention. When the Israelis entered the camp and shelters of Miyye wa Miyye they gathered all the men together, tied their hands behind their backs and made them run the three kilometers to the playground of the American school. The first man was disabled, and another one blind. We held a demonstration from Miyye wa Miyye to the UNRWA office in Sidon; then we went to the mosque, where we made a call for the youths who had been taken, we knew not where. There was also the burning of Miyye wa Miyye camp in 1982. The Lebanese forces, the Phalangist, were responsible after the Israeli army had settled at the camp. Miyye wa Miyye camp is made up of two parts, an upper part and a lower part. The inhabitants were expelled from the camp and part of it was set on fire. I remember I stood on the roof of our house which overlooked the camp and saw what was happening. People started running and another woman and I ran to the Israeli governor in Sidon and I told them we didn't want a repetition of the massacres of Sabra and Shatila in Miyye wa Miyye. A soldier came and put his hand over my mouth, telling me to be quiet. I told him, 'Go and see what is happening in Miyye wa Miyye'.

The woman who was with me was Palestinian of Jewish origin. When they said, 'Only one of you goes in to the military governor, the other stays outside,' she told them, 'I am Jewish' So they allowed her in. They told me, 'Go, nothing will happen'. When we returned, the camp was on fire, but most people had left; only those who had been hit or wounded remained. You know what weapons the Phalangist used? Sticks with nails hammered into the ends, and hoses. You got the feeling somehow that everything had been planned. The lower camp was destroyed, all of it burned, and afterwards they swept it away. But they had taken all the young men, there were none left in the camp. Young men from the Phalangist continued to beat people – among them your mother, Basma, and Umm Hussein, God rest her soul.

Basma: My mother is still blind to this day from the blow.

Kananah: They treated people badly. They told us that the Phalangist were coming to set up a base at the school and we were afraid because of what had happened at Sabra and Shatila. The rumour spread that the people in a certain house were being slaughtered; we were reliving the massacre, but it did not happen. The Phalangist had erected a checkpoint on the road to the camp. I remember there was a group of young men and women whom the Phalangist fired on but without hitting anyone; on the other side were the Israelis.

We had no money, so Abu Maher sent me 5000 liras, telling me to distribute it to the wounded. I distributed some and then went to Mohammad Salameh and told him we didn't have enough weapons. We bought rifles – imagine, hunting rifles! But how were we to get them into Miyye wa Miyye camp? A young man bought a crate of vegetables and put the rifles beneath them, the vegetables on top, and took them on foot from Sidon to Miyye wa Miyye. At the same time, during the invasion, some people, because they were afraid when the Israelis entered, threw their weapons down next to our house. I heard them and, with the help of a few young men in the camp, we hid the weapons in the water reservoir and the UNRWA bathrooms. We used these weapons in 1985. After they were retrieved from their hiding places, I cleaned them at my house. We had lookouts in front of the house, girls coming and going and men inside cleaning.

The Phalangist were getting ready to attack. We women went and brought first aid material and gathered together, preparing and sterilizing gauze, establishing a clinic. And then the battle commenced in the camp.

Basma: For the first three days no one came; we worked alone. We would go into houses under the shelling of the camp to collect food from the fridges and distribute it. In the end we went to the houses of those who kept hens and retrieved the eggs from under them and boiled them for the young men.

There weren't any people there – none. We were four girls and, in all modesty, I tell you that we were the reason for the steadfastness of Miyye wa Miyye and, consequently, the reason for the steadfastness of Ain al-Hilweh and for the prevention of its fall and the fall of Sidon. Why? Because the young men had run out of bullets, and the last Dagtaryef [a light machine gun], which Abu Youssef got for us, he threw at us and said, 'Girls go! The Dagtaryef is rusty, it doesn't work.' We were stubborn and refused to go. If we had left, the young men would also have wanted to leave, but they were ashamed to do so while we were present and determined to stay. There was no food, we would go back to the fridges and bring food; there were no sandbags, we would make sacks and fill them with sand; the weapons needed cleaning and working. We would fill the guns with bullets for the men; do everything for them, so they wouldn't retreat. And so we persevered. After three days we got reinforcements and the work started seriously.

Kananah: The hardest phase, I swear to God! Until now some sounds I hear remind me of the sniping which was aimed at us for 24 hours wherever we were. There was ammunition, diesel, medical treatment and food, all [being managed] together. The rats were at our feet.

Basma: What's important is militarily how we fought; the men were under the leadership of Radwan. This young man, Radwan, should be a military official. All along the Lebanese front we had no leader or guide or anything. Radwan formed a group and they fought alone. He was hit, poor man, and he suffered. Militarily there was very good internal organization. The example of Miyye wa Miyye became a role model for all Palestinian camps, from Ain al-Hilweh to Beirut.

Amneh: I still feel it now. During the final phase of the war of the camps in Beirut, there was no diesel, no food, nothing. The hospital would continue to function to help people. We would look for wooden sticks, firewood. A handsome young man of 23 came and asked me: Sister Amneh, what should I do? We would divide the work, so I told him we needed firewood because it would run out soon in the hospital. He went to bring wood and was shot and killed by a sniper. I felt I was dying; I cried for a whole week and kept saying, 'I am the cause of his death!'

Kananah: The human aspect during the 1982 invasion … We were introduced to a nun called Nabiha at the Najdeh society in Monsignor Gregoire Haddad's Lebanese social movement. Nabiha invited me to go and discuss matters with her and this ended with them supporting us financially, the families, the young men. I would go and collect the money – how did we distribute it with the Israelis still in the camp? Anyone distributing money was accused of being with the resistance, with terrorism. So I would wear pajamas with a robe over them at night, this wouldn't draw attention even if the Israelis saw me and I put the money either in my pocket or under my arm. I would knock on the door and say, 'This is help for you; don't open your mouth. If you talk, the next time you will not receive help.' We worked for about two or three years. I would go from Miyye wa Miyye to Alia doing the same thing. We distributed the salaries in Ain al-Hilweh and we communicated with some sisters in Tyre who would distribute to the families of the detained men. The invasion ended and no one knew that this distribution had taken place. But it was a very rich experience, without former planning – necessity is the mother of invention. We would speak about the camp, the invasion, the detention of the men, and the burning of the camp to the delegations and reporters who came.

Jehan: Delegations would come?

Kananah: Delegations came: Norwegians, Swedes, Russians, and French.

The Phalangist once made an explosion in the garage. The Israeli army came with an ambulance bearing the Star of David. When they asked what was going on, we told them, 'You know our men have been captured and therefore you must protect us'. The officer said, 'Take some weapons'; we said, 'Why should we – you must protect us. An army that occupies a country must protect the women and children. No, we don't want weapons.' When he asked who was wounded, we said no one. We did not want the Israelis to help us: we helped our own wounded. We in Miyye wa Miyye lived days of fear and terror. We would be told to shut our doors at 6 o'clock and go to bed – we were forbidden from going out.

Basma: We would be asleep at night. Our windows are made of glass in the camp and our doors have no locks, so we would close them with stones. Sometimes we would wake in the night and be shocked to find the Phalangist at the glass windows. We and the village and Miyye wa Miyye were all one family. But new faces appeared whom we did not know and when the inhabitants of the lower camp were attacked, it was the people from the village itself who did it. The lower camp knew all the people of the village, who was who, this one the son of so-and-so, etc. – they were the ones holding the sticks and whips to beat us.

Kananah: They were mixed with the strangers. After the victory of our young men, we entered the villages and saw the equipment and fortifications there. We felt these preparations must be three or four months old, because they had made passages/tunnels in the valleys and prepared beds inside. We saw things we didn't expect to see: 'We and you are friends, we are close, we are brothers,' they said; and yet they killed the young men right in the middle of the camp and we and you meant nothing! This is Israeli planning. The executioners are the Phalangist but the planning is Israeli.

Jehan: They didn't think they would be pulling out; if there had been no resistance they wouldn't have pulled out. Do they always take revenge against the resistance?

Everyone: All the villages of east Sidon ...

Kananah: It became normal. I remember the story of the destruction of Ain al-Hilweh camp in 1982 [when the Israelis carried out a massive aerial bombardment of the camp, causing heavy casualties]. We had Norwegian journalists in Miyye wa Miyye and they wanted to go to Ain al-Hilweh. I told them, 'Let's not go – we can see it all from Miyye wa Miyye'. We stood in a certain area of Miyye wa Miyye and saw Ain al-Hilweh before us, flattened like a playground. No stone remained unturned. The Norwegian journalists left, and then after eight or nine months they returned. We stood in the same place and they could not believe that this camp had been rebuilt at a time when the men were still imprisoned. They said that if they hadn't come and taken pictures and someone told them this, they wouldn't have believed it.

This is a big change for woman: she became both man and woman, responsible for the house, building it, and providing for its needs. The resistance came, but there were no plans for how people would persevere. The women would travel to Damascus to get the salaries for the families of the martyrs and prisoners, and the allowances for the full-timers, and they would be killed by Israelis on the road – they would die with the money in their possession.

Basma: The morals of some of these women were called into question. A woman from Miyye wa Miyye, Myassar Zeidan, who was one of those transferring the money, was killed by her relatives. Her husband's brother and others swore that when they went to bury another person above her after fifteen years they found that her body was still the same [i.e. uncorrupted]. The sheikh said that we shouldn't bury anyone over her, so they closed the grave and buried the other body elsewhere.

When they saw this thing they said the woman had been done an injustice. Before that they would write stuff on the walls about her, and her son, God rest his soul, would erase what they had written when he passed by. Her husband was in Fatah, but he couldn't stand up for her because all his relatives were against her.

My parents were understanding. I will tell you how they began in Miyye wa Miyye, how the Fatah movement began there. After the camps were liberated from the oppression of the Deuxieme Bureau, a group of young men, and with them a Lebanese doctor called Nazih, founded the organization in Miyye wa Miyye. I was 12 years old at the time when my brother Omar (I am the sister of Omar Antar) began with others to organize and mobilize. I became one of the children who joined the Flowers (like scouts).

I do not wish that my life was outside the resistance, or that I was not Palestinian. I have travelled a lot and met many people. I travelled to the Soviet Union, but on a scholarship, not through the Women's Union. My brother was also there as head of the Students' Union. I worked as a doctor in education, and they sent me on a course. I worked with the Women's Union in erasing illiteracy and it was very successful.

You asked about religious organizations, there are no Islamic groups in Miyye wa Miyye, only Hamas.

The Round Table discussion was held in Ain al-Hilweh camp, Sidon, in September 2007.

185

13.

ISSAM ABDUL HADI
(Deceased 2013)

Issam Abdul Hadi was a founding member of the PLO in 1964. She became a member of the Palestinian National Council that same year. Issam was also a poet. She held other positions: Secretary of the Arab Women's Union-Nablus till 1969; Honorary President of the Pan Arab Women's Union from July 1981; Vice-President of the International Democratic Women's Union from 1981 to 1992. She was President of the General Union of Palestinian Women from 1965 to 1990.

Issam Abdul Hadi reminds us how, as far back as 1948, Palestinian women were playing an important role in resisting the occupation, but the dispersal of the Palestinian people and, sometimes, ideological differences limited their advance. Because women's rights were not supported by judiciary courts, their liberation was not achieved.

WOMEN'S STRUGGLE

The Revolution has gone through stages (with ebbs and flows) and, consequently, so has the social situation of women. During a good stage, everyone wanted to participate; man, woman, girl, boy, member or non-member, organized or not, within or outside the uprising — all struggled with enthusiasm.

In reality, we had authority in the camps in Lebanon, but there was not enough pressure to improve women's situation. Let us say there were certain traditions that were overthrown, and this was to the benefit of women and the Revolution and to society as a whole. At the beginning of this transformation the man of the house would

187

complain then, after a while, enthusiasm caught on. The situation of a girl was not like before when, after finishing her education, her only job was housework etc. Now, she could participate fully in the Revolution. The situation in Lebanon was similar to that inside the Occupied Territories. However, in time of revolutionary recession, we see women's role getting smaller, but let's say that at least she made a start!

Women began their advance a long time ago. After 1948, educated women were the ones who helped their family, furthering their role within it. Women played a very advanced role at the beginning in resisting the occupation and later in resisting the conspiracies; they also had their part to play in the uprising [Intifada].

The old traditions which did not favour women were annulled by the circumstances of resisting the occupation, and by the uprising in the homeland especially. The same thing happened in the Palestinian camps in Lebanon. From 1969/70 until 1982, what limited our advance was the fact that we were scattered throughout different countries, along with a lack of discipline [on the ground], and sometimes ideological differences.

Unfortunately, there were no local Palestinian judiciary courts; there was a Revolutionary court, but that was more for military matters and other important things. There was no pressure on the man who oppressed his wife; no pressure to prevent him insulting the dignity of women, or to help her gain her rights, whether in motherhood, or in making a proper living. Some attempts were made, but not enough to make the man who oppressed his daughter or sister or wife stop such behaviour. We will not be convinced that we are developing, advancing and delivering our message until Palestine is liberated. Women deserve better recognition. But we do not want to underestimate our achievements.

Women's International Presence

The first achievement on a world level was the Mexico Conference of Women denouncing Zionism. This was a world victory. We proved with the support of the Soviet Union that we had a political presence, and could influence decisions at Arab and international conferences. It is enough that our union was nominated for the presidency in the Pan Arab Women's Union, but I only accepted honorary presidency.

The United Nations International Women's Conference in Mexico in 1975 saw the first established Palestinian victory. We cannot forget the withdrawal of the Arab, Muslim, African, non-aligned and socialist states from the auditorium at the beginning of the Israeli delegation's speech (given by Leah Rabin). The Americans were among the most important states along with The Netherlands, Israel, Britain and other European states, which did not withdraw. But the auditorium was close to empty. The UN General Assembly endorsed the final document of the conference equating Zionism with racism. And so we proved a main and political presence within the framework of the world democratic women's union, which had an advisory role in the United Nations and was one of the most important progressive women's gatherings in the world. Palestinian women and the Palestinian delegation began to have a real political presence at international seminars.

Women's Liberation

The support of the PLO for women's issues could have been stronger, it's true. But political issues and concerns had priority. We used to say that the homeland and human beings were liberated, but we neither retrieved the land nor did the human beings achieve victory. There was consensus regarding the importance of women's rights and their demands for a place in the leadership of the union. Women essentially proved their presence by their actions. They initiated activity among the masses and the general public, but without changing the personal status law. However, there must be legislation, because without legislation men won't comply.

The most essential right women need is legislation on divorce because it gives Muslim women some assurance. Tunisia is an example of a country where women can ask for divorce. Then comes the issue of early marriage. Protecting her children is most important, the right of the mother to look after her children at least until the ages of 15 to 18, when they then can choose one or the other parent. But for the child to be taken from the mother and she forbidden to see the child and look after him or her, or to go to another woman or to a harsh father, this is unacceptable. There should not be multiple wives without a valid reason. Family violence should be avoided because children are the victims.

Inheritance must be equal. Many fathers are careful on this issue and by playing around with the law they can ensure equality. Nevertheless, the text in the *Quran* stating that the male has the right of inheritance twice the amount of the female is very difficult to change. Indeed, in some cities and villages, and in the desert, a woman would of her own free will give up her share to her brother. This is not because of religion; it goes back to tradition. If a woman wants to hold on to her rights, she should. She must not sign them away. There must be legislation to protect her. If there is a will, then everything has a solution.

Extracts from an interview published in the Arabic book *Palestinian Women in Lebanon: The Resistance and Social Changes –Live Testimonies of Palestinian Women in Lebanon 1965 – 1985*

GUPW administrative council meeting, 1981

14.

Mai Sayegh
(Extracts)

A writer and poet on the Palestinian National Council, Mai has published a novel and the story of the siege of Beirut. She is an active member, of the General Union of Palestinian and Jordanian Writers. She was secretary of Fatah's Women's Office, a member of the Revolutionary Council, and Secretary General of the General Secretariat of the General Union of Palestinian Women from 1974 to 1985, as well as serving on the PLO's Central Council during the same period. From 1979 to 1985, she was a member of the Permanent Office of the International Democratic Union. Her interview reveals the relative independence of the Women's Union from the institutions of the PLO, and how it managed to make its own decisions despite not being given the representation it was owed and deserved.

From the beginning, my personal experience was widening and my role in the Fatah movement opened doors that had been closed regarding my direct knowledge of the miserable social situation of women, dependent and subordinate, who were having to make great efforts to deal with life. The situation of women was and still is very complicated; it is the main issue whose solution is necessary to solve other societal issues arising from the rules, concepts and ideologies that have prevailed for centuries.

The experience of the Palestinian resistance in Jordan did not have time to mature, but it undoubtedly was able to play an important role in the formation of the mass psychology of the Palestinians in general. The resistance opened doors for women which had been completely closed and enabled them to enter the workplace and participate in voluntary work. The influence of this period shows in the popular songs at weddings and in popular political feelings during main events — this notwithstanding that the period following the departure of the resistance was very harsh on Palestinian society, dominated as it was by fear, terrorism and defamation of the resistance.

THE STRUGGLE OF PALESTINIAN WOMEN

The struggle of Palestinian women did not start with us. They participated effectively in earlier Palestinian revolutions, including in the military and political organization. Palestinian women won a distinguished place within the Revolution because of their serious daily struggle. The General Union for Palestinian Women (GUPW) formed a real struggling presence for Palestinian women at the level of the Revolution and Palestinian society — but that was not enough.

The war in Lebanon placed a huge burden on women and they had to struggle on more than one front, making their way in a difficult social reality and harsh political circumstances. During the siege of Beirut we formed a joint committee with the Lebanese women to work in the camps and neighbourhoods. We also formed the Lebanese-Palestinian National Committee for Relief and Aid from representatives of the parties and factions of the Lebanese National Movement and the Lebanese and Palestinian popular unions and social institutes. Our GUPW was the basis for this work.

THE REFUSAL OF THE UNION TO COMPROMISE

The regression and dispersal of the Revolution, followed by its acceptance of the imposed solutions (Oslo) and the tragedies that ensued, hit deeply. The Union rejected the political compromise from the start, its position having been solid since Camp David and the conspiracies that followed. It paid a big price for this in neglect and sanctions.

In 1974, we held the second Congress of the GUPW which included female representatives of the branches of the Union from Arab countries. Delegations from the Arab and international unions were also present, such as the Women's International Democratic Federation (WIDF) and the Pan Arab Women's Union. The Congress rejected the political formula adopted by the leadership, which accepted a Palestinian state on any land that was liberated. The Congress considered this an acceptance of the political compromise and an abandonment of the programme of total liberation. Discussion took up most of the time of the Congress and women's issues received scant attention.

The GUPW was punished for rejecting this political scheme that opened the door, later, for political settlements.

THE LIBERATION OF WOMEN

Before 1975, the cause of women's liberation received little attention from the Union, apart from when reading periodicals we used to receive from democratic countries and different unions around the world. Then the UN declared 1975 to be International Women's Year. Our membership in the Women's International Democratic Federation (WIDF), and then joining the PLO as an observer member at the United Nations, enabled us to start working on an international level.

In fact, we were merely an extension of the political organizations. Our continuous presence in the enemy's line of fire did not allow us the luxury of posing the issue of the violation of women's rights and the cause of their liberation, which had imposed itself on us from the beginning. The leadership neglected it, even when we organized a special seminar to discuss the matter with them.

But the question kept arising about the situation of women, their rights, and the position of the Revolution on their equal status. In truth, we did not reach a convincing answer, because the liberation of the land did not necessarily liberate women, and the Revolution had no real position, apart from words of encouragement and compliments on special occasions, despite our achievements in many fields. We achieved essential victories on the international level and secured recognition of the justice of our cause. We succeeded at the UN International Women's Conferences in 1975 in Mexico, and in Copenhagen in 1980, to get the support of women from around the world and won the decision to condemn Zionism as a racist movement, equal to apartheid. The decision was passed by the General Assembly of the United Nations in 1975. Unfortunately, it was later rescinded after [the PLO leader] equated the struggle of the Revolution with terrorism, in Geneva in 1988.

On a theoretical level we did not escape the limits of a patriarchal system which is no different (except in some trivialities) from patriarchal systems in the Arab world. Any change or development of ideas within this system does not happen quickly but needs a long and serious struggle. National independence does not necessarily include social liberation and a change in human values.

We could not fight the women's struggle when we were constantly facing the circumstances of war, threatened by acceptance and refusal, the issue of recognition; we were always looking for our legitimacy inside the revolutionary movement.

Even the size of our representation in the Palestinian National Council, which we demanded should be in proportion to our numbers and effectiveness, took years to resolve and we remained weak. We were very convinced that we had to enter the decision-making hierarchy so we could pose our causes. The submissions would be in writing to the presidency of the council and then voted on in the articles of membership – but our suggestions on women's issues were neglected. Though our representation increased, so did the number of National Council members. Abu Ammar, God rest his soul, kept drowning the council with more supporters of the hot issues he was trying to pass by a show of hands.

It was not possible for the leadership of the Union to shape an ideological view or a concept for the liberation of women, for the Union is formed mainly from the different Palestinian factions and these all differ on how to treat the cause of women. Palestinian society embraced and accepted with respect the roles that women played in the Revolution, which contributed to establishing positive values – though they were not yet enshrined in law. We tried several times to open a broad discussion with the advanced cadres from the different organizations, and we held special seminars with leaders of the organizations. When the discussion reached the need to put the conclusions into effect in laws and directives giving women their rights and protecting them from the practices and traditions that oppressed and humiliated them, the excuse was that this cannot be accomplished because of the absence of land. Laws cannot be applied in the Palestinian Diaspora because of the other laws that apply in the country of refuge, and we don't want a collision with personal status laws. Of course, we had to commit to the stance of the Revolution, and our political role always took priority, for we did not join the Revolution for the sake of liberating women but faced the issue when it came our way. Our struggle mainly focused on freedom and participation in the Revolution as a part of the cause of the liberation of society as a whole.

The Importance of the Women's Magazine

For the GUPW journals are very important. *The Revolutionary Palestinian* magazine was published in Amman, and then there was one issue published in Lebanon in our name, without our knowledge. We decided to ban its distribution. Our political position was the reason that the leadership would not support any further publication of our magazine without their interference.

The first interview was conducted in Paris in 1995 and a second one in Amman in 2008.

Extracts from an interview published in the Arabic book *Palestinian Women in Lebanon: The Resistance and Social Changes –Live Testimonies of Palestinian Women in Lebanon 1965 – 1985*

GUPW delegation to Vietnam, 1980

15.

INTISSAR AL-WAZIR/UMM JIHAD

Umm Jihad comes from Gaza where she was living at the time of the interview. Her husband was martyred leaving her with three sons and two daughters to bring up. She has held many positions of responsibility within the Fatah organization, amongst them as a member of the Central Committee and, in 1980, of the Revolutionary Council. She was a member of the Administrative Committee of the General Union of Palestinian Women-Syria, and of the GUPW's General Secretariat (1980-85), later becoming GUPW President. From 1994 to 2004 she was Minister of Social Affairs in the Palestinian National Authority (PNA). She is also President of the Institute of Martyrs' Families. Her interview concentrates on the difficulties women had in attaining positions of responsibility within the Revolution, and on the situation of widows following their husband's martyrdom and their entitlement to a widow's pension.

THE FATAH MOVEMENT AND THE PARTICIPATION OF WOMEN

There were two currents inside the Fatah movement. One believed in the role of women within the movement and the other that she should work only at home. We were able to promote the cause of women, though it took great effort. At the Fourth Congress of the movement in 1980, six of us ran for the Revolutionary Council – I was the only one to succeed.

THE WOMEN'S UNION AND WOMEN'S LIBERATION

If it were not for the Union and its struggles, women would not have reached the level that they did. Women were absent from the scene. It was difficult to propose a programme for women with the complexities of the issues of the Revolution and the daily conflicts and battles that it faced. It was difficult to propose issues related to the ideology of women and our vision to liberate them. But we struggled for women to take their natural role in political decision-making and to participate in the political institutions. We thought that such participation would develop their social situation.

But this participation is still weak. For example, there is no woman on the PLO Executive Committee. Even in the wider circles of the PLO, the participation of women in advanced positions is weak. In 1988, the number of women on the National Council was 30 to 33 out of 350 to 400 members, in other words about 10 per cent.

Everyone asks, what is the guarantee that we do not become another Algeria? I think we have more women who are aware and educated now. The social development which occurred inside the Revolution could have been much greater. But I think the position of women was not unified. For example, during the Fourth Congress, when we wanted to nominate someone to Fatah Revolutionary Council, we were told to agree two candidates and nominate them. Why should we agree only two, while all men are eligible? Women must struggle and not be afraid of defeat.

During the period of armed struggle and national liberation it was difficult to propose values and laws when we were not even on our own land and unable to execute them. Women's struggle is more likely to begin when women inhabit their own land. Women in Lebanon are subject to the laws of the Lebanese Government, in Syria to the laws of the Syrian Government, in Jordan to the laws of the Jordanian Government. It is not possible to struggle to improve the social laws of countries in which you cannot change the constitution.

Introducing some laws which might be applied to the cadres was difficult. The cadre would reject interference in his divorce or marriage. This was the problem.

THE INSTITUTE OF MARTYRS' FAMILIES: SOCIAL PROBLEMS

The basic problems we used to face at the Institute of Martyrs' Families and their social issues were usually between the wife and the husband's family, especially regarding the 'pension'. In our system the pension goes to the wife and children; consequently, the husband's family sometimes wanted to ensure the wife's failure of duty in order to deny her custody of her children, so that the pension would go to the husband's family. But we took a firm position on this issue and were compassionate towards the wife, always standing by her. We were thus able to keep many families united and the children stayed with their mother.

If the wife re-married and was able to keep her children, we would allow her to continue receiving the pension; but if she left the children and the children went back to the father's family, we would stop paying the wife a pension. In most of the marriages that took place among martyrs' families, it was traditional for the wife to marry her husband's brother so that he helped provide for the children, and we would not cancel the pension which was for the wife. If she did not want to marry her husband's brother, we would stand by her, protect her, and prevent her brother-in-law from blackmailing her. If she married a stranger, and her new husband agreed to keep the children with him, we would continue to pay the pension. Very few of the wives of martyrs re-married – not more than three per cent.

MULTIPLE WIVES IN THE REVOLUTION?

We do not have legislation regarding multiple wives. For example, if a fighter left his wife and children and re-married, we would investigate the family and submit a request to the military administration asking them to cancel a part of the fighter's salary for the benefit of his first wife – a specific part of the salary, sometimes half. Having more than one wife was not forbidden, but neither was it a social phenomenon. The biggest problem facing the fighters which led them to taking multiple wives is that they were far from their families for long periods. For example, if the wife were inside the Occupied Territories and the husband outside, he was unable to enter, and she was unable to come out, so he would have to re-marry. But when the wife was present with her husband, there was no reason for him to take a second wife. Within the Revolution these issues were not discussed.

VISION FOR THE FUTURE

The vision for the future has to be explored on the ground with no fast decisions. We must reach a state of awareness and democratic dialogue towards a conclusion that would guarentee rights for women – where these rights do not contradict Islamic law or heavenly laws in the land of Palestine.

The interview was conducted in Amman, October 1994.

Extracts from an interview published in the Arabic book *Palestinian Women in Lebanon: The Resistance and Social Changes – Live Testimonies of Palestinian Women in Lebanon 1965 – 1985*

Sabra and Shatila massacre, 1982

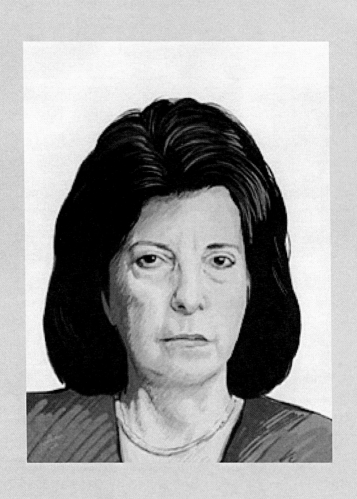

16.

Bayan Nuwayhed al-Hout

Writer, historian and professor, Bayan al-Hout was born in Jerusalem in 1937. She has a PhD in Political Science and was Professor of the Palestine Question and Middle Eastern Studies at the Lebanese University (1979-2001). Member of the Arab National Conference since 1992, she became a founding member of the National Islamic Conference in 1996 and of the Al-Quds International Institution in 2000. Among her many publications is Sabra and Shatila: September 1982. *She is a widow and a grandmother. Her political initiation was through the Arab Baath Socialist Party, the most active organization at the time, rather than through social work. She was instrumental in setting up an oral history project and her achievements are testimony to her long involvement in the Palestinian struggle.*

My testimony stems from personal experience. I do not distinguish between the work of women and men in life in general, whether it is a political activity or something else in which they are jointly participating. For Palestinians in the Revolution, when men and women were separated, it would be for security reasons. When we gathered as women alone it was for security reasons. It was impossible in the 1950s and '60s for a meeting to be held in a house with women and men talking politics. If a security person or indeed anyone knocked on the door during one of these meetings, the woman answering would say that there was a birthday party or some such celebration going on. That's why candy and music were always on hand for camouflage. The time and place of these meetings differed. A meeting could not be held again in the same house for four to six weeks.

My familiarity with the Lebanese arena goes back to 1959, specifically the summer of that year when we came back to settle in Lebanon. I found the work in Lebanon different from Jordan as there was more freedom, and the meetings between men and women were easier than they had been in Jordan. Back then I did not have separate work, Palestinian or Lebanese. I was working through an Arab party, the Arab Baath Socialist Party. Our political meetings concerned everybody. We were in university student circles, Arab students from all groups, from all Arab countries. There was no issue of discrimination about nationality. This was out of the question. The work was 100 per cent political. We were not concerned with social issues at the time.

In the early 1960s, when I was working with the party in Lebanon, I was also working in journalism. I was a party member and I would write political articles and social reports.

We founded an association for working women. It was rarely heard of because it withered after a short while. We, Baathist girls, founded the 'Association of Working Women' with other friends. It was not affiliated to any party. Its goals were general. I was first introduced to the Tal al-Zaatar camp through the association. We visited the camp several times to establish literacy classes for women.

I left the Baath party in 1964 when I started another political activity with the Palestinian Liberation Front: Road of Return. There were many Palestinian members and possibly other Arabs, but the majority were Palestinian. It was an undercover front which women also joined. This group of women would meet alone without men, sometimes for security reasons and sometimes to discuss issues that men could not discuss or that did not concern them. You may find it strange, but I am proud to say our leader in this circle was Samira Azzam – God rest her soul. Samira Azzam was a great person and she wrote short stories. I interviewed her when I was a journalist and met her in many literary circles, which is why I was surprised that she was involved in this secret political work. Shafiq al-Hout was the major person in this organization; he founded it but refused to take any title such as president or general secretary. He believed in group leadership.

One day Samira asked us to get ready to enter the camps. One of our sisters insisted on doing it alone, to surprise us. She was almost arrested. The Lebanese intelligence bureau instantly called the PLO office saying that someone from our side had entered the camp and asked on what basis that was. There was an official investigation. However, our work in raising political awareness continued. We did not intend to carry out social work such as establishing kindergartens or hospitals. But by talking and holding seminars we helped women to become politically aware.

Other work was women's work in a wider sense within the framework of the PLO. We supported the commandos through socio-political work. Activities to help them were not restricted to raising money and bringing gifts, but involved establishing a relationship with them, the idea being to let the commandos feel that people supported them. A project called 'the Fedayee (freedom fighter) sweater' was set up where women would knit or buy the sweaters. (The knitted ones were preferred.) The young men were very happy with these sweaters and felt the importance of having them. Many women wrote them letters and gave other gifts. We felt their need for many things, among them pyjamas, sweaters, shaving kit and books. These would all go to the area of Al-Aghwar at the time. We would share the responses we received with the women. The phase of the 'Fedayee's sweater' was a beautiful one, and sisters from many organizations and parties set up similar projects, which greatly pleased me. The 'Fedayee's sweater' committee continued for many years.

Then I moved to the Union for Palestinian Women, but the experience was short lived as the Lebanese University had opened a Department of Graduate Studies at the Faculty of Law and Political Science, and I registered for higher studies immediately. With three children and higher studies I couldn't go on working in the Women's Union. Many sisters co-operated together and did 100 per cent women's work.

I knew the reality of women not through the popular committees but through the press, through many journalistic reports. We were the guests of working women. Despite the difficult situation, I witnessed their enthusiasm and positivity, their desire to develop and learn. I followed up the Women's Union and know they did a very good job. They established several kindergartens and attended to women's education, their economic situation, and the economic situation of the family.

IMPORTANCE OF ORAL HISTORY

In summer 1982 I was teaching at the Lebanese university. I wanted to set up an 'Oral History' project inside the camps, beginning with the displacement of 1948. It was not social work. I was doing this project with Edward Said. At the time he was the chairperson of the Institute of Arab Studies in America and he had asked me what I would like to do. So I told him I had an interest in oral history but, although I had approached the Institute for Palestine Studies and the Research Centre and the media department of Fatah, all of them had their own reasons for not wanting to support the project. Edward Said told me this could be a one-person job and he would send me some books of oral history that had been researched by one person. So he sent me three or four books and the one I was most interested in was about the Revolution in Spain in the 1930s – a subject I had already studied. In my doctoral thesis about the political leadership of Palestine I interviewed many people, not all of them appearing in the text. But I saw the importance of oral history is that sources and information

210

would be checked and corrected. I wanted to start in summer 1982, but then came the Israeli invasion of Lebanon. As the bombardments became heavier and we were in a shelter in Beirut, I decided to turn the project towards the war of 1982. I thought maybe we would do something about the Israeli invasion. But there was no chance to discuss this because, after the invasion, the massacre of Sabra and Shatila took place on 16 September. It is the tragedy of my life that I did not know about it until September 18, the third day when it was all over. This bothered me a lot.

Sabra and Shatila Massacre

Why couldn't I enter the camp? Because we were weak. Why did the massacre happen? Because we couldn't protect the camp. This matter effectively devastated me. Maybe the Sabra/Shatila project began by coincidence. It was not a decision at all. Shafiq was travelling, and people would come and talk and tell me their problems and I would record them. When they told me their stories, I would say, 'I haven't read this in the papers'. Journalism comes to me from abroad. My friends were sending me stories, but not the story of, say, this or that specific woman. I felt that the tragedy was far greater than reported. So after a few meetings I started recording the testimonies. The project turned into one about Sabra and Shatila. I should have entered the camps, but I was not allowed in. They might turn a blind eye if you entered other camps, but Sabra and Shatila was difficult – you had to enter through an army checkpoint.

Three-quarters of the personnel at this army checkpoint were from the Lebanese Forces [involved in the Sabra/Shatila massacre]. I entered the camp 12 times, but from different places. It was not possible to do all the interviews inside Sabra and Shatila without being discovered. In such a case we would have been finished.

When I did enter the camp, it was to record the realities of the

211

massacre. Of course, destruction is destruction, but there was psychological damage as well as damage to the houses. Sabra and Shatila affected me greatly. Even now I remember the destroyed streets that I passed through with a girl who lived in the area – we walked a long distance until we reached the Sports City.

It took almost three hours to walk through Shatila main street on the last day of the massacre, as people were frequently stopped and interrogated. People had been kidnapped on the streets. People had also been kidnapped off the streets. The third day of the massacre was the worst. It was a Saturday. Kahan [the Israeli judge in charge of the enquiry into the massacre] said in his report that it was over by morning. That is not true. They were still killing people in their hiding places until noon that day. Personally, I am still affected by all this. I cannot see an armoured vehicle or bulldozer without remembering Sabra and Shatila, because the bulldozer had such an impact at the time. Three years passed and I entered the camps freely in the spring of 1984 because the political reality in Lebanon had changed after February 6 [Intifada in West Beirut]. We entered the camps and did a big field study, distributing questionnaires. I had a work team of volunteers, all from Sabra and Shatila, most of them Palestinians, but also some Lebanese who contributed and helped a lot. We finished the study in about 40 days. I went back to writing, and we made other visits to the camps later on.

Politically, nationally, on a civilizational level, patriotically and socially I was very disturbed by the mass grave in the camp, which was left unattended for so long. For political reasons the Lebanese state initially forbade the erection of a memorial for several years. Then Ahmad Sa'id al-Khansaa, mayor of Ghobeiri, which is a patriotic municipality, along with all the members of the municipality, fulfilled his promise to erect a memorial.

The Palestinians in the camps held on to their identity. We must not forget that there is a distinguished role for women and this was evident in the study. To begin with, it was the women who held out in the camp, not the men. It is true that the Lebanese allowed the refugees of 1948 to stay, but there were people who left with the fighters [when they were forcibly evacuated]. And others who fell as martyrs. So this is why it was the women who actually held out in the camp. In my field study there was only a small percentage of displacements from Sabra and Shatila.

After 1982 there was dreadful negligence. Families were in a terrible situation. There should have been much more attention paid to the economic situation. They [the PLO] were supposed to help people stand on their feet and provide them with jobs. Lebanon itself was in a bad situation. Palestinians were forbidden to work. There were huge difficulties after 1982. I call them the years of oppression.

There is an old saying I like and have benefited from, which is quoted at the end of my book. It is by Rabbi Abraham Herschel: 'When a crime occurs, those guilty are a few individuals or groups, but everyone bears responsibility ... in a free society some are guilty, but all are responsible'. If we want to apply this to Sabra and Shatila, those who carried out the crime are well known: the Lebanese forces and their supporters from other Lebanese militias, the Israeli army who had the place under siege and facilitated, maybe drove, the Lebanese to do it. All is possible. There is a big responsibility on those who executed, sponsored, and opened the way. But I think the main responsibility was that of the Palestinian leadership and the leadership of the local organizations – on all of us and on me as a human being. I am a citizen and I swear to God I, too, am responsible.

We should have said the camps were definitely in danger [following the evacuation of the PLO and fighters from Beirut in August 1982]. We should have thought of this. Who were we leaving them to? Didn't Abu Ammar speak about the security of the camps? Didn't the Americans say the camps were under their protection? We saw the multinational forces leave. Who were they leaving the camps to? It is strange we didn't think about it. An American friend of mine asked me why did the American forces [who were there as part of the multinational force] leave so soon after the exit of the fighters? Of course, I told her I had no documented proof, but I believe maybe they wanted to please the Israelis in some way. Time may show that the massacre was set up, along with the entry into West Beirut of Israeli forces. It could have something to do with the assassination of Bashir Gemayel [leader of the Lebanese Forces who became President of Lebanon in 1982] – I cannot know. There are signs that say there are connections. Nevertheless, in terms of responsibility, when they left we should have thought about the camps. The greater responsibility no doubt is on the leader and the leadership.

WOMEN'S STRUGGLE AND LEADERSHIP

There's no question that Palestinian women did not get the right to reach leadership positions. But, historically, Palestinian women were among the first Arab women to take political rights without demanding them and without demonstrations. It is rare to find an Arab country where women acquired their rights without campaigning. In Lebanon there were demonstrations. Likewise in Egypt there was a huge women's movement; and before that there was Huda Shaarawi. Palestinian village women were admirable in their struggle and perseverance, helping the men in the fields, raising their children at home, carrying produce on their heads and selling it in the city. Even now in Jerusalem and Al-Khalil, I am happy to see such women sitting in their embroidered dresses, which they probably made in preparation for their weddings. We, in Beirut, used to embroider silk dresses and sell them. We were proud that we struggled and wore a Palestinian dress to a party. I am talking about groups; that's why the struggle of Palestinian

214

women is continuous. In the Gulf they were afraid to employ young men, as they might be politicized but girls cannot be politicized, so they would accept female teachers rather than males during the 1950s. Women saved their families economically. Was it possible that women were going to train to use arms in Al-Aghwar [the Fedayeen military base]? Their families accepted with time. The first Palestine national conference in 1964 was attended by many women. There were no general elections. Who decided that they could attend? Men, thanks to Ahmad al-Shuqairi, God rest his soul, and the advisory committees. There were nine or ten women *vis-à-vis* approximately less than 300 men – which was good for that period! There were many Arab countries then where the political rights of women went unrecognized. Now there are female Palestinian ambassadors in many countries.

Interview conducted in Beirut, September 2007.

Bayan Nuwayhed al-Hout, Sabra and Shatila, September 1982

17.
HADLA AYOUBI
(Deceased 2018)

Born in the 1940s, lawyer Hadla Ayoubi was originally from Jaffa in Palestine. Once a secretary to Libyan royalty, her job was public relations director of the Palestinian Red Crescent Society, of which she was an executive bureau member. She was also a member of the Palestinian National Council. We learn from her interview of the work of the Palestinian Red Crescent and the role of foreign doctors who came to the aid of the Palestinians during the Israeli invasion of Lebanon in 1982. The horrors of the Sabra/Shatila massacre are described. A woman of strong character, Hadla had no qualms acknowledging that she was more or less married to the Crescent.

I am Hadla Subhi Ayoubi, born in Jaffa, studied in Jerusalem at the Nuns of Sahyoun School, graduated with a GCE certificate. I am one of a family of six children: three boys and three girls. As Palestinians we were scattered throughout various countries. For a while my parents lived in Amman, but we moved a lot from one country to another. After leaving Jerusalem in 1967 we moved to Lebanon, then to Libya, then back to Lebanon and, finally, back to Amman. When I graduated I worked as private secretary to the Queen of Libya, living with the family for four years, during which time I was always saying I wanted to study and continue my education, and in the end I did. I left and went to the Arab University of Beirut where I studied law from 1962 to 1966 – and I did well.

My father had practised law in Amman where we were living at some point. My dream was to become a lawyer and defend people's rights. So when I graduated I trained for two years in my father's office, took the oath and started practising. But I didn't find what I had been dreaming of, so I began to look elsewhere. A friend in Lebanon, Dr. Nabila Nashashibi, suggested I work with the Palestinian Red Crescent Society (PRCS) and there I met Dr. Fathi Arafat, chairman of the Society at the time, who put me in charge of public relations. That was in 1979. I am by nature neat and well organized. After working a few months at the Crescent I became an observer member on the executive bureau. Dr. Fathi wanted to encourage women and increase the number of women members on the executive bureau: then there were only three. I remained director of public relations until the Israeli invasion of Lebanon in 1982.

When we were in Lebanon many Lebanese came to the centres of the Palestinian Red Crescent Society because during the Civil War the Lebanese Ministry of Health was not functioning, so all those who could not pay for treatment would come to our clinics.

As a testimony to history, I want to say that it was felt at the Crescent that a big event, war, was coming, and the medical sector and clinics were well prepared, as if for an invasion. During this period there were always events in the South, constant attacks, until the Israelis finally invaded Lebanon in 1982. There was shelling and we were on the front lines in Ghubayri, and we had to move. Dr. Fathi was far sighted in moving us quickly to Hamra so we would be further away from the bombardment and also be able to inform the outside world what was happening. We stayed there until the agreement for the PLO to leave Lebanon was reached. The multinational forces entered. During this time all our up-front facilities had been working.

The Red Crescent worked quickly and achieved a lot. We had a clinic in every neighbourhood, and there was much co-operation with the Lebanese health committees. But the most important position for us was an underground hospital at the Center of

Theology in Hamra and this played a big role. I would like to salute all the European committees who were in solidarity with us and helped us at that time because, although the Arabs wished to help, they could not enter Lebanon. The foreigners managed, with difficulty, playing an extremely important role. The largest numbers who came during the invasion and worked mainly at the Theology Center were the Norwegian doctors, surgeons and nurses, alongside our own young people. When the decision to pull out from Lebanon was taken and Dr Fathi was forced to leave, he told us that he was leaving the Red Crescent in our care, that is with Wijdan Siyam, myself, and foremost with Dr. Azmi al-Jishi. It was following the departure of the PLO [as stipulated under the agreement with the Lebanese] that the massacre of Sabra and Shatila took place.

SABRA AND SHATILA MASSACRE

We were in Hamra at the time and news filtered through that something was about to happen. We had a number of foreign nurses and doctors at the Gaza Hospital which was inside Sabra refugee camp. They left and came to Hamra and, as public relations representative in constant communication with them, I asked what was going on. They said that their embassies had told them to leave as the situation was unstable, that the multinational forces, who were there for our protection, had pulled out and this was an indication that something was about to happen. It seemed that their embassies had told them to pull out in advance of the massacre.

I told them I appreciated that their embassies were concerned for their safety, but that if they left we would remain unarmed with no protection and no medical assistance. I felt very emotional but at the same time I told them calmly that, in the end, it was their decision and we did not want to put them in danger, but this was the test for it. They met and decided to return to the camp. Among those who returned were Doctor Swee Chai Ang, Doctor Charles

Morris and Nurse Ellen Siegel. Aziza al-Khalidi was the director of Gaza Hospital at the time. These medics resumed their roles at the hospital. It was afterwards that the massacre took place.

THE HEROIC MEDICAL TEAM

The medics had returned of their own accord, with no pressure from anybody. They felt that if they pulled out they would be leaving the Palestinian people at the mercy of the perpetrators. Swee, Siegel and Morris were all detained as they were walking through the camp; they saw the bodies of the slaughtered women and children at the side of the road and the bulldozers burying bodies in hundreds. The first official to make public this information was the Norwegian Ambassador, who warned that something momentous was going on in Sabra and Shatila camp. Later, the medical team courageously testified before the Kahan Commission [set up following the Israeli invasion to investigate the massacre] about what they had seen. The Kahan Commission found Sharon responsible [Israeli commander, later Prime Minister].

At that time, Doctor Azmi, Wijdan Siyam and myself were all under the protection of the International Committee of the Red Cross (ICRC) – protection that was not out of fear for our souls but to enable us to move around.

PEOPLE WITH SPECIAL NEEDS

Another foreign doctor, Jean Calder, a rehabilitation specialist and humanitarian worker was working with children and people with special needs through entertainment and games in order to rehabilitate and integrate them into society. An activist with the Australian Palestine Solidarity Association, she visited us at the Palestinian Red Crescent Society in the 1980s. At the time we had a boy called Hammoudi from Tal al-Zaatar who had cerebral palsy staying at the Nazareth Hospital in Ghubayri along with a blind girl, Dalal, and another child called Badr. Jean decided to join the Crescent where she played an honourable role. At Haifa Hospital in Burj al-Brajneh camp we had a centre for those with special needs, mostly the wounded; there was also a division for children. At the time, Jean was at Akka compound opposite Sabra-Shatila camp, sheltering underground with ten children with special needs, when the gunmen entered their shelter. The children witnessed everything, unfortunately. The gunmen raised their weapons at them, but left without firing. The children were rescued by the ICRC and taken to hospital suffering from shock and trauma

After 1982 the Crescent took the children to Cairo where Jean was able to take care of them – it was as if she had adopted them. She later lived with them in Khan Younes in the southern Gaza Strip, where we have an excellent rehabilitation centre, aiming to integrate them with other children.

Jean later wrote a book about her experiences in Lebanon and the situation in Gaza. She was made a Companion of the Order of Australia for her humanitarian work.

ENTERING SABRA AND SHATILA

When I and my colleague Wijdan Siyam entered Sabra and Shatila with the ICRC immediately after the massacre, the dead bodies were still on the ground. We went on the third day. The representative accompanying us advised us not to get too close, saying 'what you see will live with you for the rest of your lives'. We saw from afar and saw enough to send us both into shock.

People persevered. They returned to the camp. Imagine, before sunset they would not go out of their homes – even if a cat moved outside they would not go out. They lived in terror, but despite that they would not leave the camp because part of the plan of the

Lebanese Forces was for them to leave Lebanon. Even those who left for just two or three days, some to the Red Cross in Ras Beirut, returned – they all returned. They wanted to keep their identity and, in any case, where would they go? They wanted to preserve what they had. The Gaza Hospital was no longer a hospital. Displaced Palestinian families and Lebanese lived there – Lebanese people in the camp were also killed.

We opened our centres and put the Red Cross sign over the Gaza Hospital. The Red Cross representative installed a communications system with the Hamra office for immediate notification of any events. There were two operators of the wireless system. Following the massacre, on at least half a dozen occasions, people would suddenly cry: 'The Lebanese Forces are here,' and they would run away from the camp in fear. One morning I was going to Gaza Hospital with a representative from the ICRC, a young Dutch volunteer, and a young Lebanese woman. As we stood there someone shouted: 'the Lebanese Forces have arrived'. I cannot describe the scene of people running — you know how sheep run when they are taken for slaughter. The Red Cross representative told me to take the young women and run. We ran, and the people ran, but the ICRC representative stayed. When we got to the end of the camp we waited outside. After half an hour they announced that it had been a false alarm.

Afterwards, the Red Cross representative told me he would have been among the first to be killed, since he had lost his identification card and had no proof that he was a Red Cross representative. We cleaned the Gaza Hospital from end to end and the staff returned to work, gradually regaining confidence, and we re-opened all our centres. Thank God, we had support from people around the world, some of whom would come and visit us. I was extremely affected by this.

I wanted so much to stay in Lebanon but, unfortunately, I have a Jordanian passport and my residence permit had expired and the

Lebanese authorities would not renew it. So I had to leave Lebanon. By then I was in a state of collapse. I had done what I had to do during those events.

STEADFASTNESS DURING THE SIEGE

I want to tell you about a nice incident. Dr. Fathi, God rest his soul, would go from Hamra to Ghubayri to visit Akka centre and sometimes I would go with him. One day during the siege, we were at Cola roundabout and there was heavy shelling on the areas we were going to in Ghubayri. I was afraid but didn't say anything. After a while Doctor Fathi remarked that the shelling was very close, so we should return to Hamra. Of course I felt relieved. The next day there was a further bombardment and Doctor Fathi said, 'come on, Hadla!' I said, 'I am sick, I cannot, I have stomach ache'. He said, 'Hadla, I am telling you, come on, we are going to Ghubayri'. I am grateful to him because if I hadn't gone that second time I would have lived in fear all the time. He broke my barrier of fear with an order: 'we must go to Akka Hospital in Ghubayri'. We went and there was no heavy bombardment as there had been the day before. Of course, this period was not easy for anyone and the Palestinian people were emotionally exhausted from constant shelling. Towards the end of the invasion the shelters were bombarded with smart bombs. Some of those in the shelters of the Theology Medical Center were burnt. I would refuse to go to a shelter, preferring to die above ground. During the invasion I documented every school, church and cultural centre that was shelled. A group of Italians collated it all in a small book. I consider this book, of which I have a copy, to be important documentation of everything that was targeted.

Every individual who lived through that period should record his/her experiences and all these writings should be gathered in a book because it is an important part of our history. The perseverance of people, their courage, their humanism, all is important; there were honourable roles, there were people who gave a lot.

When most people had to leave Lebanon [i.e. those Palestinians who had not been living in Lebanon before the early 1970s], communication with the Crescent was difficult, so we had to maintain our relations with institutions such as the International Red Cross and the Crescent abroad, and with the international unions and solidarity committees. We opened an office in Greece, which was very supportive. I lived there for eleven years with two Greek secretaries and I still keep in touch with them — in spirit they were Palestinian.

After 1982 and the Sabra and Shatila massacre, the activities of the Crescent decreased for a short while. Then we returned as we were getting support from outside. But of course it was difficult for specialized doctors to enter and movement was difficult. However, the Lebanese Red Cross took an honourable position in support of us. When the invasion took place, Alexandra Khoury, the President of the Lebanese Red Cross, God rest her soul, was still alive. When the Crescent was threatened with closure, she said, 'close the Crescent? Who will look after the Palestinian people? The Crescent will keep working for the people.'

WOMEN'S RIGHTS

Maternity leave in the Crescent was 70 paid days and thereafter an hour daily for breast feeding until the baby was a year old. But most Crescent centres had kindergartens.

Men accepted me as their supervisor, although it bothered them when I was quickly given a leadership position. But once they got to know me, it was ok. I used to work from the morning until ten at night; we would work our shift, but then there were always delegations coming to the PLO. People were respectful. I never felt that a man, whether a nurse or a doctor, tried to insult me because I was a woman.

Among the achievements of the Revolution has been the transformation in the role of women. I became a member of the Palestine National Council when I joined the executive bureau of the Palestinian Red Crescent Society, which chose the members with the approval of Abu Ammar.

MY OPINION ON MARRIAGE

I never married. A woman cannot choose, you know; you cannot choose the man you like, who suits you. I say: either a good marriage or no marriage. I didn't feel I had to get married. There are many women more educated than me, who believe they have to be under the protection of a man. I personally never had this feeling, thanks to my mother. She never told us we should get married, like some mothers do. You could say I married the Crescent! There are men who are not comfortable with a woman of strong character.

The interview was completed in Amman, March 2008.

18.

KASSEM AINA

Living in Beirut, previously from Safad in Palestine, Kassem Aina is director general of Beit Atfal Al-sumoud, established by the General Union of Palestinian Women, and a member of its Administrative Council. Formerly, he was a researcher in the educational social division of the PLO Planning Centre. He has worked with the orphaned children of Tal al-Zaatar, and also with Lebanese orphans. He laments the change in the attitude of Palestinians in Lebanon post-1982, noting that before the Israeli invasion there was more solidarity. He notes, too, that the Sabra/Shatila massacre was not the only massacre of Palestinians in Lebanon to take place, and that the massacres at Tal al-Zaatar and elsewhere were not given the same prominence. He regrets the wave of emigration of Palestinian males that followed 1982 and the effect this has had on marriage prospects of women left behind.

Beit Atfal al-Sumoud (BAS) is the Institute of Tal al-Zaatar. In 1976 the General Union of Palestinian Women's General Secretariat founded the Institute and named it Tal al-Zaatar in honour of the camp's defenders, fighters and martyrs and to embrace the orphaned children of Tal al-Zaatar. Some time later a number of children in similar situations (loss of both parents) were also taken in from other camps. They were from Jisr al-Basha, Rashidiyeh and Burj al-Shimali camps. From its foundation it did not differentiate between Palestinian or Lebanese orphaned children.

The experience of BAS is unique. The children live together in the Institute as a family, every eight to ten children from one family or extended family live in an independent apartment, but they eat, play and practise their hobbies together as one big family. In addition, we believe in integration so children go to ordinary UNRWA schools.

BAS has passed through many phases, but the most important human element were the women, mainly acting as substitute mothers, playing a vital role in raising the children by compensating emotionally for the loss of their biological mothers. Maybe the image of the father was represented by the schoolteacher, the driver, the cook, or the 'dabkeh' folk dance trainer. Women at the Institute also worked as social workers, doctors, kindergarten teachers, and nurses. From 1984, the social workers at BAS had a huge national role in the absence of the resistance.

Women at the Institute taught history to the children, keeping the memory of their camp alive; they contributed to celebrating national occasions. This reminds me of the Sabra and Shatila massacres and how, in 1984, '85 and '86, young women of Shatila would go to the cemetery carrying roses in remembrance of those massacred, only to find it had become a rubbish dump, the gate of which was locked.

The Institute is proud of the role played by its young women, especially the first groups. However, there is a big difference between the experience of the first generation and the current one. The former lived during the period of the nationalist rise in the camps, the experience of the Revolution and its achievements. The difference now is that this latter generation, men as well as women, did not experience an atmosphere suitable for national mobilization in the camps and even in the institutions.

Kassem Aina

PALESTINE IS AT THE HEART OF OUR WORK

The number of workers at the Institute is some 80 to 90 women. We work for the people, in the public interest. We have no president or general secretary – we have joint solidarity. There is a link between these sisters and the letters of appreciation they receive from those who become patrons of the children [patrons build a personal relationship with the children and support their expenses] they see during their visits. Because of the wide net of relationships they have formed internationally, most of the social workers are able to take the children abroad, where people show their appreciation for the nature of their work, and their professional and national role. This, too, is a kind of compensation not available to many women who work in other institutions.

The average age of those working here is between 23 and 45, and since the Institute's foundation men and women have held the same rights. If the woman is a widow she is treated as the head of the family.

After 1983-84, we added the child survivors of the Sabra/Shatila massacre. We had a new project called 'Making the Family Happy', which aimed at taking care of the child within their family. BAS is one of the first institutions in Lebanon to care for this aspect. We had a large building to house the children of BAS, which we had to leave after the 1982 invasion. 'Making the Family Happy' is dependent financially on the guarantor or on patronage [donations and personal relationships with the child].

Every 30 families have a social worker who knows all about each family and builds a good relationship with it, trying to solve its medical, educational and residential problems or any other associated matters. The social worker works not only with the child, but also with the family. The activities in our centres are open to anyone in the camp, but financial aid is given only to the heads of families in dire conditions. We try to take responsibility for such a family so we can reassure them that someone will take care of their children.

Since 1982, unfortunately, the situation of the martyrs' families has been very difficult. The Institute of Social Affairs affiliated to the PLO is responsible for martyrs' families. It was never as effective as it should be, with few humane relations, and mostly post-1982. The Institute of Social Affairs pays the families at the end of the month, or every two or three months – and that's it! It needs a different policy to the current one. The lucky families – those with some kind of rank – receive about 100 dollars a month.

SERIOUS PROBLEM FOR PALESTINIAN GIRLS

There are many reasons why a large number of Palestinian girls are unmarried, the main one being the economic situation. Many young men are emigrating. At one time in an area of the South there was one man to every ten women. Where are the rest? They emigrated. Sometimes, if a man doesn't marry abroad, he returns to marry a young woman from here.

After the war of the camps some young men left for Denmark and Germany. However, there is a phenomenon that caught my attention with regard to the women who married: our colleagues, for example, are all university graduates, and yet when they married, in general, they married men who were less educated than they were. I couldn't find an explanation. I can't understand a university girl, who has finished a sociology degree and is working, marrying someone who works as a driver, who would want to impose his will on her. The reason is mainly because her situation at home was difficult, so she wanted to escape. If she was without a mother and father, her brother might be imposing his will on her.

It is not acceptable for a young unmarried woman to live alone. If, due to her work, she has to move from one city to another, she lives with someone. Or two or three young women will live together – like university students. In the past, there was more Lebanese-Palestinian intermarriage and openness. Moreover, young women do not emigrate alone.

With the deteriorating political situation, social problems increased. As for so-called honour crimes, there aren't any. Divorce, yes; it is increasing, especially among the women of Nahr al-Bared. We are a society like any other: when there is poverty and oppression and fear of the future, everything becomes permissible. Ignorant and illiterate people, how can you expect them not to take drugs? People with no hope: what does it mean? How will they view life? They escape.

However, I haven't seen violent crimes of men against women. In spite of the bad situation in the Palestinian camps, the ratio of crime is very low. But if I want to make a comparison between us in 2007 and, say, in the 1970s, I would say that in the '70s our situation was much better – there was solidarity among families and at the level of the camp. Today, familial solidarity is weak, but there are societal deterrents in the sense of prevailing values in society. When an old man in the camp tells a young man 'shame on you!', it does have an effect. There is this amount of respect, but it has decreased and is decreasing further. The unity of the camp is an expression of the unity of society. For example, in Burj al-Brajneh, there are still connections between the inhabitants of former Palestinian villages that have a positive role, maintaining the solidarity of the inhabitants of the village. When there is trouble among young men, at least these connections can intervene to solve it, because in Burj al-Brajneh we don't have the 'Armed Struggle' (the police of the camps), nor in Shatila. I think solving social problems is, first of all, the responsibility of different political organizations, for example for protecting the camp from drugs, so that it does not threaten our youth. Treatment is possible, but costly; that's why we should work on the important factors of awareness and education. You need to start with the organizations

– they need awareness first of all, because it is easier to address an organized group than to address the whole camp. We also co-operate seriously with Lebanese associations in this domain; there are some cases which we turn over to them.

BAS works in solidarity and co-operation with more than 2,000 women, for example with kindergarten teachers. We help to solve legal problems. Our aim is for children to have an identity. Some widows have problems with their in-laws and we solve them via our social worker, without publicity.

We take responsibility for the children of a martyr's wife if she wants to re-marry, or if a child wants to live with their grandparents we arrange this in consultation with the mother. But as a matter of principle we encourage the wife of the martyr to marry a man who accepts her children, and this should be one of her conditions for accepting the marriage. Where there has been conflict between the woman and her in-laws, we have supported the woman. It helps that the social workers are from the same camp, as people then know who they are. Every social worker has a programme and should visit the family at least once or twice a month; but when there are problems there is no definite time limit.

SOCIAL WORKERS' LEVEL OF EDUCATION

Social workers are university graduates and we train them. Today, Palestinian women are more educated than the men. The ratio of girls' success to boys is higher. At BAS there is a continuous programme of training and qualification. There are qualifications with specialized associations and there are sessions we organize only for our cadres.

Religious Movements

There is no evidence of ex-cadres and freedom fighters, or women, joining extreme religious movements such as Salafist groups.

I distributed the book *Castro and Religion* some 15 years ago when we were just beginning to look at how we should deal with society, how we might use religion in a positive manner.

Before and After

Let us separate the two periods before and after 1982. I view before 1982 as the enlightened period, for both women and men; but after 1982 we began gradually to go backwards, to the extent that I would say even solidarity among brothers and companions has become so weak that it is only occasional. This is an objective result of people being absorbed by their own issues. It is the result of the defeat.

There were eight children, four by four, in our family. There was no fanaticism, but there was conservatism as a kind of defence of the Palestinian identity. It was very hard during that period to organize young women to go out to meetings. It was difficult even for men. I remember that in the Arab National Movement, maybe in the whole of Tal al-Zaatar, at the time when I began political work, we were only three cells. The number was small because of concern about repression from the Deuxieme Bureau. When I joined the resistance, I changed. I remember when Abd al-Nasser died, my elderly mother would go from Tal al-Zaatar to Beirut on foot to demonstrate in sorrow about his death.

Before, everyone was preoccupied. When I wanted to distribute leaflets, I would wake up at night and without anyone knowing, while everyone was asleep, out of fear that the Deuxieme Bureau would find out and come after us, I would hastily scatter the leaflets around our neighbourhood. But when the resistance emerged everything changed.

When the resistance came to the camp, it increased solidarity and co-operation among people, whatever village in Palestine they came from. A town or village would no longer meet on its own as they had done before. I remember one time at midnight we were passing through a narrow street in the camp when an old lady called to us, 'come and sit, I will make you a cup of tea'.

Too Many Massacres

Following the massacre at Tal al-Zaatar there was an attempt to gather the names of those who had been killed. But the massacre was not given the same attention that was given to Sabra/Shatila. The reason for this was that because of the Israeli involvement in the latter it was considered a war crime, while the Tal al-Zaatar massacre was viewed as an internal matter and therefore not given international attention.

There were other massacres. For example, Jisr al-Basha camp had 3,000 inhabitants, 183 of whom were killed; similarly Burj al-Shimali, but these concealed events were not documented as massacres. In Burj al-Shimali, during the Israeli invasion, 125 were massacred within minutes in the Holeh Club shelter, and the Najdeh kindergarten shelter was also attacked. These, as with Tal al-Zaatar's 2000+ martyrs, were forgotten.

Women's Situation in the Two Periods

In the period before the emergence of the resistance, families were fairly cohesive; although women did not have freedom of choice, whether in education or marriage. With the resistance came some freedom. Women joined organizations, they had a role, they worked, their education increased, they went abroad. I don't know of a single young woman who left Lebanon for her education before the arrival of the resistance. Then they began to go to the

Soviet Union to study. Two of my sister's daughters from Tal al-Zaatar went; one became a staff nurse and the other a gynaecologist. That's why these were enlightened years in women's history. Later, there was regression and women went back to being enslaved by the values and traditions prevailing in family and society.

THE PLO: SOCIAL CONTEXT AND FAMILY LAW

Theoretically, legislation is not in the hands of the PLO. Today, if a woman wants to get married she has to go to church or the law court. The Revolution helped bring out the capabilities of a woman, giving her some freedom, respecting her as a human being, ensuring she was a partner in the building of society and family. We were all drawn towards political activity; it's a short period from 1970 to 1982, and its good that these achievements took place. We made it internationally; our battle was not only inside, but outside also. I think the Women's Union played a positive role, but it was cut short as a result of the defeat. 1982 was a defeat.

MALE AWARENESS

Of course, these are my convictions. The children are grown up now. But before, I did not give my children what they deserved. I gave all my time to my work. I personally feel that I did not do enough for my children. The basic thing is how much you are in harmony with your convictions. When I was married by the Sheikh, four of my friends accompanied us. I told the Sheikh that the bond of marriage was in my bride's hand; my friends were leftists, but even so they were embarrassed. A woman is a human being like me and marriage is a partnership. Maybe if Fayzeh hadn't been so understanding of my work, I wouldn't have given the Institute so much. She bore all the responsibilities of the house;

if I succeeded in my work, it's thanks to her. I think the younger generation did not have the same experiences. The experience of the resistance benefited us a lot. We acquired new values, which weren't prevalent a long time ago. Much also depends on your upbringing at home. My father was not educated, but he had an open mind and I changed his perceptions.

This interview was conducted in Beirut, September 2007.

ACKNOWLEDGEMENTS

This book has had a long and thorny road. It wouldn't have seen the light of day were it not for the inspiration, support, encouragement and practical help I received, especially in its translation and editing.

Special thanks and appreciation are due to Rosemary Sayegh, Emeritus Professor Sami Zubaida, the writers Beverley Naidoo, Annemarie Young and Haifa Zangana. Warm thanks to my patient editor Anne Rodford and to Amal Karam, Haifa Ruhayem and Hadi Ruhayem.

I am thankful to my publisher Tony Simpson for the care and attention he has given to my book.

Special thanks and acknowledgements are also due to the talented artist, Fuad Alymani, who provided the illustrations for the majority of the interviewees. I also thank Yousef Qutob, the long-serving and renowned photographer of Palestinian activities in Lebanon. He provided the cover photo and many of the pictures inside the book.

Jehan Helou

Jehan Helou was born in Haifa in 1943. Soon, al Nakba uprooted her family to Lebanon. For long years she was a pioneer in the Palestinian national struggle and the women's liberation movement. More recently, her fervour is directed towards children's culture; she is president of the Palestinian section of the International Board on Books for Young People.